1940s

The 1947 MGTC

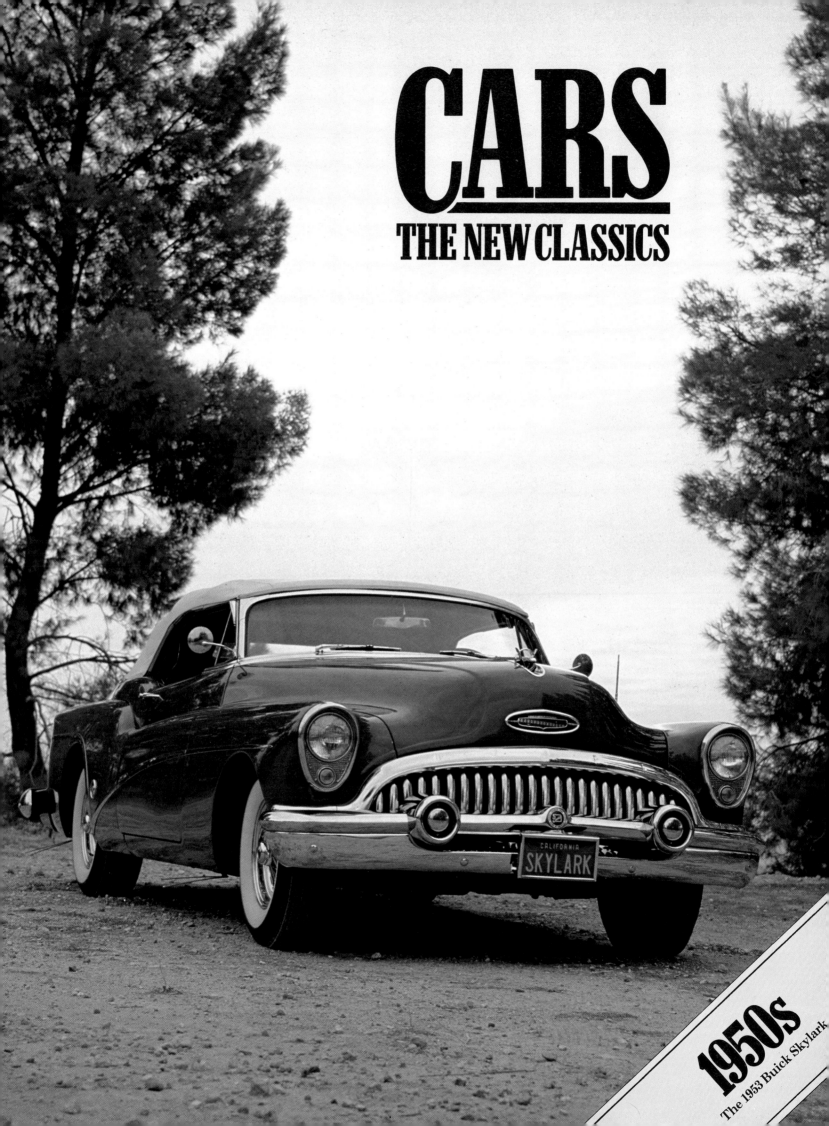

CARS
THE NEW CLASSICS

1950s
The 1953 Buick Skylark

CARS
THE NEW CLASSICS
FROM 1945 TO THE PRESENT DAY

Chris Harvey

octopus

First published in 1981 by Octopus Books Limited
59 Grosvenor Street, London W1

© 1981 Hennerwood Publications Limited
Reprinted 1983
ISBN 0 7064 1626 0

Produced by Mandarin Publishers Limited
22a Westlands Road
Quarry Bay, Hong Kong

Printed in Hong Kong

CONTENTS

1970s

The 1972 Lamborghini Countach

FIRST IN THEIR CLASS

ABOVE *The Allards, built by hand in London to accept large American engines, were among the first British cars to sell well in the USA after the Second World War. Despite their massive construction, weight was kept to a minimum on competition models, such as the J2 pictured here, by using only skimpy coachwork.*

RIGHT *One of the most advanced cars made in the early postwar years was the Italian Cisitalia, with an ultra-lightweight spaceframe and coachwork by Pinin Farina (renamed Pininfarina after 1958). This is the 202SC model made in 1948 using mechanical components from contemporary saloon cars.*

There was a time not very long ago when anything classic had to be old. In the case of the car, it had to be one made before the last great event that everyone remembered, the Second World War. However, many classic cars have seen the light of day since 1945 and we can now take true stock of ourselves in relation to that often most prized possession.

To the majority of people the car represents freedom: freedom to escape from boring routine, freedom to go anywhere at any time, freedom from the inconvenience of public transport, freedom from everything except the cost of motoring. That is why people get so intense about cars, because they are such an important part of their lives. And that is why classic cars create so much interest: because they are the very best of the bunch. To be considered a classic, a car must set standards of design and engineering above those of its contemporaries.

During the Second World War great technical strides were made, particularly in the field of transport, with the result that cars made before war broke out in 1939 now look rather ancient, while cars conceived since the war ended in 1945 appear, by comparison, quite modern. In most cases postwar cars fall naturally into four divisions: sports cars, saloon cars and convertibles, exotic cars and competition cars. Much has been written about racing cars and in recent years these have become so technically sophisticated that they bear little relationship to road-going vehicles. Therefore this book concentrates on cars that can be driven on the road.

Inevitably a few classic cars stand out from the rest and justify the status of first in their class, either because they set new trends in design and engineering, or simply because they are outstanding in both appearance and performance.

It was not surprising that, after the wholesale destruction of the Second World War, most manufacturers had to rely on prewar designs to get their production lines rolling in 1945. In that year, provided you did not expect a new design, the MG TC was the undoubted classic sports car: there was hardly a nut or bolt on it that was new, just a body 10 cm (4 in) wider than the MG TB, which had been discontinued when war broke out, and minor modifications to the rear suspension to make it easier to maintain than the TB. This product of the biggest sports car factory in the world at Abingdon, Berkshire, in the heart of rural England, was everybody's idea of what such a car should be. It seemed to be capable of almost anything: racing, rallying, popping down to the shops, and it was without peer when it came to courting; Prince Philip drove one before he married Princess Elizabeth in November 1947. It was cheap and charming, with a good-looking open two-seater body, and bounced along on its cart springs: but it held the road so well that a whole generation of racing drivers cut their teeth on it, including the United States's first World Champion, Phil Hill.

It was in America that this British anachronism had its biggest impact. Although only 2000 of the 10,000 examples made went to the USA, the MG TC started the postwar craze for British sports cars that was to grip the United States for 35 years. Surprisingly it also helped to launch the

The Volkswagen Beetle, which went out of production as recently as 1978, dates back to a prewar design by Ferdinand Porsche. More than 15 million were manufactured of which this one, made in 1947, was the first imported into Great Britain. The distinctive split rear window of this model can just be seen.

*Road and track racing after the war was dominated
by the sound and fury of Ferraris. These Italian aristocrats
were made in only small quantities, almost invariably with V12
engines, and often with lightweight coachwork as on
this 1951 212 Barchetta model.*

world's most popular car, the Volkswagen Beetle, in what
was to become its largest market, America. To establish the
Volkswagen in the USA, the importers insisted that dealers
who wanted an MG should take a Volkswagen as well. As
a result, the German 'people's car' went on to overtake the
prewar Model T Ford with production figures in excess of
15 million. The conventional front-engined, ladder-framed
MG and the rear-engined, air-cooled, platform-chassised
Volkswagen saloon might have been capable of only
around 130 km/h (80 mph) from four cylinders, but they
were seemingly indestructible classics.

The Volkswagen's designer, Prof. Ferdinand Porsche, was
as famous as the car itself and founded a dynasty that was
to produce one of the world's most popular series of sports
car, the Porsche. The first of these extraordinary, buglike
devices was built from old Volkswagen parts at Gmund in
Professor Porsche's native Austria in May 1948. This
beautifully streamlined little car, designated Type 356,
stayed in production with many modifications, including a
larger engine, until 1965.

The other great classic sports cars of this immediate
postwar period presented contrasts just as great as the
sophisticated, all-enveloping, Porsche Type 356 and the old-
fashioned MG, with its 'Le Mans' slab tank attached to the
rear, separate wings and running boards. The Allard, which
was built in the back streets of London with a massive
tubular chassis and American V8 engine, was as brutal as
they come: a postwar reincarnation of the Bentleys of old
which had been described as 'the fastest lorries in the
world'. The Allard, at its best in J2X form with a 160 bhp

Cadillac engine (the most powerful American unit available
at the time), had scanty bodywork with mudguards like
those of a bicycle and, because of its low overall weight and
enormous power, was capable of astonishing acceleration. It
was as strong as a truck and there were solid grounds for
suspecting that many of the parts came off lorries: its
creator, Sydney Allard, used to recondition Ford trucks
during the war!

Enzo Ferrari's first creations after the war had an equally
solid chassis, with 'unforgiving' roadholding, but there was
nothing crude about their mechanical attributes. They had
marvellous V12 engines with five-speed gearboxes that gave
them searing performances in skilled hands. The first of
these Italian aristocrats that could be bought by a
sufficiently wealthy man in the street was the Type 166 with
a 2-litre engine; later models, such as the 2.6-litre Type 212,
easily exceeded 195 km/h (120 mph).

These were really thinly disguised racing cars, unlike the
Cisitalias made in Turin by the Italian industrialist Piero
Dusio in the late 1940s. His aims were always firmly in the
direction of competition and he eventually bankrupted
himself building a Porsche-designed Grand Prix car.
However, his coupés were practical road cars because they
incorporated modified Fiat components. They used
advanced lightweight spaceframes (so called because the
network of tubes from which these chassis were built meant
that the frame featured more space than metal when viewed
as a whole) and, in the most notable cases, bodywork by
the famous coachbuilder Pinin Farina that set a trend
followed by other stylists for many years. These wonderful

Cisitalia coupés (pronounced Chisitalia) showed what could be achieved using production car components as a basis.

It was in these early postwar years that work began on one of the most famous sports cars manufactured in Britain. The gifted stylist William Lyons was building the first Jaguars based on prewar SS sports cars and saloons. However, the name had to be changed because of the emotions raised by those sinister initials after the war. The engine was also altered: Lyons needed more power to make his cars world beaters, and his brilliant team of engineers, led by Bill Heynes, perfected the first mass-production twin overhead camshaft engine, the legendary Jaguar XK that is still being made in modified form in the 1980s. The combination of a soundly engineered but conventional chassis, with Lyons's timeless styling, and the enormous power of the new engine, led to the Jaguar XK120 of 1948 which was to take the car world by storm.

This classic sports car was only the beginning of the road as far as Lyons's ambitions were concerned. He was using it merely as a testbed to attract publicity for his new saloon: the Mark VII Jaguar which was to be the world's first 160 km/h (100 mph) luxury liner. Needless to say, this saloon, introduced in 1950, was just as successful, establishing new standards for others to follow.

The most extraordinary feature of all Lyons's products was their low selling price. Intensely competitive pricing was possible because of a tight-fisted control of component costs. This led to volume sales that enabled Jaguars to be manufactured at a low unit cost which still produced a profit. (One of the few cars that could surpass the Mark VII Jaguar in terms of performance and comfort was the Bentley Continental, which cost four times as much.)

Equally great strides were being made among the small cars, and the first of Alec Issigonis's masterpieces, the Morris Minor, was introduced in 1948. This was the car that should be remembered as the British Volkswagen in that it fulfilled the people's needs so well. If anything, it was more of a classic than the Volkswagen in that it had exceptionally safe handling, an area in which the German car was never strong. One of the greatest motoring writers of the day, Laurence Pomeroy, said of the Morris Minor: 'It handled better than any of the contemporary Grand Prix cars'; this was frightening when you consider that they produced something like 400 brake horsepower (bhp) against the 24 of the Morris Minor!

Just as Morris set new standards for small cars with the cheap Minor, so too did the British sports car manufacturers in the early 1950s. Two deadly rivals, Healey and Triumph, announced in 1952 the world's first cheap 160 km/h (100 mph) sports cars, the Austin-based Healey 100 and the Standard-based Triumph TR2, designed to increase the British penetration of the American market pioneered by MG and Jaguar. These were simple, straightforward cars that were notable for performance in relation to their price. MG followed up three years later with the MGA, of which even more were sold.

LEFT *The Jaguar XK120 was a truly great classic, capable of more than 195 km/h (120 mph) and costing less than £1000 on introduction in 1948. This is the famous 1950 competition model, driven by Ian Appleyard to numerous international rally victories, preserved in its original form.*
OVERLEAF *The Morris Minor was the first of two remarkable mass-market cars designed by Alec Issigonis. This is an early side-valve split-screen model built in 1949; it was extremely durable and had excellent roadholding. His next great work was to become even more famous: the revolutionary Mini of 1959.*

The Chevrolet Corvette introduced in 1953 featured glass-fibre bodywork and rapidly became accepted as America's only true sports car. Its styling and specifications changed over the years, often being available with the most powerful of the giant Chevrolet V8 engines. This is a 1967 model.

This attack on the American market, which amounted to about 30,000 vehicles a year, was but a fleabite to the American giants, who were topping eight million cars a year by 1955, but it was sufficient to inspire them to make their own sports cars. The first of these, which still remains the most significant, was the Chevrolet Corvette, developed by a European engineer named Zora Arkus-Duntov, who had been involved with Allard. The Corvette's most notable attribute, apart from a large helping of horsepower from a variety of big engines, was its glass-fibre body. The Americans were pioneers in the successful use of this light and corrosion-free body material which had been developed in California for the hulls of speedboats.

These cars were unsophisticated compared with the sports models being made in Europe. Mercedes-Benz in Germany produced a real classic in the spaceframed 300SL, which had such a deep side framework that it needed upward-hinging gullwing-shaped doors for easy access; whereas on the delightful Giulia, the Italian firm of Alfa Romeo used unitary construction (the combination of body and chassis as one lightweight unit) with the company's small twin overhead camshaft four-cylinder engine and excellent suspension.

Alfa Romeo's rival in Italy, Lancia, was making the most progressive car of the early 1950s in terms of design: the Aurelia. Saloon versions of the Aurelia featured pillarless construction of the combined body and chassis and they were all powered by the world's first V6 engine. This configuration was to be adopted during the next 30 years by Ford, Maserati, Peugeot, Renault, Volvo, Fiat, Ferrari,

General Motors and Mercedes. The Aurelia was also one of the first cars to use radial-ply tyres and independent suspension all round with a rear-mounted transaxle: a combination of gearbox and final drive that reduced unsprung weight and allowed a more even distribution of weight within the car's structure to give better handling. In fact, both the aerodynamics and roadholding were superb and in coupé form the Aurelia B20 vied with the Cisitalia for the title of the world's first Grand Touring car.

However, French engineers left everybody standing with the Citroën DS19 introduced in 1955. This exceptionally smooth saloon had a very advanced hydraulic system which allowed the use of self-levelling suspension, automatic jacks, and power steering and braking. Despite having an antique engine, the DS19 had such good aerodynamics that it was capable of cruising at high speeds with good economy on the long open French roads.

Soon after, the Suez crisis of 1956 cut supplies of oil to Europe and petrol rationing was re-introduced in many countries, including Great Britain; and naturally there was a great demand for economical cars. Among the first classics to emerge in a crop of such vehicles was one of the best-looking GTs ever made, the Lotus Elite of 1957. This tiny car was a gem, with its beautifully streamlined bodyshell made entirely from glass fibre, which was a revolution in itself. The suspension, based on that of the contemporary Lotus Formula 2 racing car, ensured excellent roadholding. The 1216 cc Coventry Climax engine was available in various stages of tune and most Elites were capable of 160 km/h (100 mph) and 7 litres/100 km (40 mpg). High standards of maintenance were needed for this Lotus, however, and it soon gained a reputation for unreliability. Nevertheless, it remained one of the most significant and delightful classic cars, an example of what can be achieved by brilliant design rather than by brute force.

Meanwhile Ferrari was dominating the larger, and more expensive Grand Touring (GT) classes with a variety of cars powered by V12 engines varying in capacity from 3 to 5 litres. The smaller cars in this range were the most popular, particularly the 250 GTs built from 1956 with bodies designed by Pinin Farina, who had been responsible for the Cisitalia. Despite being 'softer' machines than the earlier, savage, competition Ferraris, these GT cars gave excellent performances that were equalled only by the Jaguar XKs, before the British specialist sports car manufacturer Aston Martin produced the DB4, its version of a Ferrari, in 1958. The DB4 was similar to a Ferrari in concept with a body designed by Touring of Milan. Its all-alloy six-cylinder twin-cam engine gave it a similar 225 km/h (140 mph) plus performance to that of the Ferraris, but its race-bred handling was generally considered superior.

At the opposite end of the scale, Alec Issigonis completely changed the face of motoring with the Morris Mini-Minor in 1959. It is doubtful whether any other car has had such a powerful influence on motoring since: not only was the Mini (which was also produced in Austin guise) cheap and economical, but it offered exceptionally roomy accommodation in a very restricted overall size, with the additional advantage of excellent handling. With its revolutionary space-saving transverse engine and front-wheel drive for better roadholding, the Mini was such a brilliant design that it became a household word, applicable to seemingly everything from computers to girls' skirts. The handling of these amazing little boxes on wheels was so good that competition versions were soon dominating the smaller classes in saloon car racing, and even winning international rallies.

In the same period, Jaguar developed a new line of unitary-construction small saloons into their 'ultimate', the Mark II, powered by any of three versions of the XK engine. The most powerful, the 3.8-litre unit, was similar to the one that had given the marque a string of successes in the world's most prestigious car race, the Le Mans 24-hour endurance event. This compact Jaguar saloon, which weighed little more than an XK sports car, offered an incomparable combination of comfort and very high performance at an exceptionally low price: so much so that it sold extremely well and became instantly beloved of businessmen (who appreciated its comfort and economy) and bank robbers (who appreciated its ready availability and performance).

In 1961 Jaguar followed this up by producing one of the fastest and most spectacular sports cars ever made, the E type based on the company's Le Mans-winning D type racing cars. Like the Mini and Mark II Jaguar, this car became symbolic of a generation freed from the constraints of postwar austerity.

All sorts of classic cars emerged during this time of relative prosperity. An Italian tractor magnate called Feruccio Lamborghini felt piqued at being kept waiting by

---

The Lancia Aurelia of 1950 set a new style for Grand Touring cars with lightweight unitary construction, a high-performance V6 engine, gearbox in combination with the final drive, and all-independent suspension. This 2500 GT version was driven to victory by Johnny Claes in the 1953 Liège-Rome-Liège rally.

The Lamborghini Miura was as fearsome as the fighting
bull it was named after. This mid-engined Italian masterpiece
introduced in 1966 was capable of nearly 290 km/h (180 mph), thanks
to the tremendous power of its V12 engine. It held the road well,
provided the driver was sufficiently careful to handle it properly.

Enzo Ferrari when collecting his latest GT, and decided to build his own cars. The results were some of the most extraordinary exotic cars ever seen. The first was the 350GT built in 1963 and designed chiefly by former Ferrari men. As Ferrari used the symbol of the prancing horse, so Lamborghini chose the bull. Then Lamborghini produced an even faster car in 1966, the mid-engined Miura, capable of nearly 290 km/h (180 mph). This magnificent, aggressive-looking machine bore a close resemblance to two of the greatest racing cars of the day, the Ferrari P3 and the Ford GT40. However, the Lamborghini that followed in 1967, with a similar V12 engine, was like nothing else on earth: the Espada was a full four-seater (rather than a two-plus-two) and capable of nearly 260 km/h (160 mph)! Ferrari, meanwhile, continued with wildly exciting, but conventional, front-engined machines, the most significant of which was the 1969 280 km/h (174 mph) Daytona.

However, that same year Ferrari brought out the Dino 246, a small and extremely attractive mid-engined coupé. This was a very popular car and soon became a rival to Porsche's classic GT, the 911, which had been introduced in 1964. A replacement for Porsche's 356 series, the 911 was to become renowned for its versatility. In varying forms, it won all manner of events both on and off the road and provided many owners with rapid and reliable motoring.

In Great Britain the last of the traditional Rolls-Royces had been produced in 1966 and a unitary-construction Rolls, the Silver Shadow, was selling well. It was left to Jaguar, however, to produce the best saloon car ever in 1968, the XJ6, which set new standards in handling and quietness for a volume-produced car at the by now

traditional bargain price. Three years later, in 1971, Rolls-Royce survived bankruptcy to introduce the elegant Corniche convertible, based on the Silver Shadow, just before Jaguar brought out its long awaited XJ12 saloon. This 12-cylinder version of the XJ6 was soon to be voted

Best Car in the World by an influential panel of judges appointed by *CAR* magazine. There was simply nothing else in the same class that could offer 225 km/h (140 mph) performance with superb handling, and carry four people in such comfort. The only problem with the XJ12 was its tremendous thirst for fuel, which became more serious with the world's first oil crisis in the winter of 1973.

However, Porsche was able to counter this major setback, and the increasingly stringent American exhaust emission laws, with a turbocharged version of the 911, the 930, which was to become one of the most practical exotic cars and is still in production today. After Lamborghini brought out its greatest car, the fantastic, futuristic Countach, an equally stunning car appeared in Great Britain. Aston Martin, having survived repeated financial crises, introduced the Lagonda in 1976. This super-luxury car, with a very potent V8 engine from the Aston Martin DBS, is without doubt one of today's most attractive cars.

The Rolls-Royce Corniche became the property developer's dream in 1972. As Britain went through a period of great prosperity, there were long waiting lists for this car which was a real status symbol, because it was the most expensive and luxurious example of the standard Rolls-Royce range.

SPORTS CARS

ABOVE *The extremely low Marcos sports car produced in the west of England started its life with a marine ply hull! Its light weight, excellent handling and superb aerodynamics gave it an outstanding performance with a variety of engines. This 1971 model has a 3-litre Volvo engine.*

RIGHT *The HRG 1500s produced in small quantities after the Second World War were like relics of a bygone age. They were beautifully built, but retained the qualities dear to the hearts of prewar enthusiasts, such as a beam front axle and cable-operated brakes. Nevertheless they performed with great distinction in international rallies.*

ost of the classic sports cars made after the Second World War came from Great Britain. This was because the far bigger American industry concentrated on building saloon cars and trucks, and the industries of other European countries suffered more heavily from the ravages of war. Initially, the MG TC was the outstanding product, but there were two similar cars made in far smaller numbers that have every right to the same classic status: the Morgan and the HRG.

Morgan had made its name before the war with very light three-wheeler cars powered by a variety of motorcycle engines that gave them a tremendous, if somewhat perilous, performance. This was a very conservative company, sticking to time-honoured methods of construction in a small works at Malvern in Worcestershire. When Morgan's first four-wheeled cars were introduced just after Christmas 1935, they were along similar lines to the contemporary Singer and MG sports cars except that they featured independent front suspension, the origins of which could be traced back to the first Morgans in 1910. This Morgan continued in production almost unaltered after the war, using a specially made 1267 cc Standard four-cylinder engine that gave it a similar performance to the MG TC, about 130 km/h (80 mph) flat out. The Morgan's price was virtually the same and it was produced in two- and four-seater forms. It could not be considered a serious rival to the MG, however, because it was produced only in small numbers. At one time four were being made every week, which was just enough to keep the trim department fully occupied from Monday to Friday if all the cars were two-seaters. If one of the cars was a four-seater, the trimmers had to work overtime on a Saturday morning!

The HRG was built in a similar way, using a Singer engine of either 1100 cc or 1500 cc but, like the MG, it had a beam front axle. There was nothing remotely modern about the HRG: it even had old-fashioned cable-operated brakes and bore a close resemblance to the vintage Frazer-Nash sports car with which its builders, E.A. Halford, G.H. Robins and H.R. Godfrey, of Surbiton, Surrey, had been associated before the war. Around 200 were made between 1946 and 1955, when demand fell off, including a few aerodynamically shaped coupés and modern prototype sports cars. Like the Morgans and MGs they had an excellent sporting record in rallies and circuit racing.

The far larger Allards were also produced in small numbers along similar lines, using a variety of American V8 engines and carrying either touring or closed bodywork. Whereas the 1500 cc HRGs were capable of up to 145 km/h (90 mph), the Allards with the larger engines of up to 5400 cc could exceed 160 km/h (100 mph).

The next notable sports car to emerge in Great Britain was the 1948 Jaguar XK120. This used the new 160 brake horsepower (bhp) 3.4-litre XK engine in a shortened version of the Jaguar Mark V saloon car chassis. However, the body, with its beautiful, long, low, sweeping lines, was entirely new and had a timeless elegance. This combination of beauty, price (extraordinarily low at £998), and a performance in the realms of the fantastic, made the XK120 one of the most significant sports cars to be produced after the war. Its top speed of 200 km/h (125 mph) could only be equalled by the outright racing sports cars, produced in very small numbers at six or seven times the price. In fact, a slightly modified prototype achieved an astounding 212 km/h (132 mph) and tremendous publicity.

That year also saw the introduction of a particularly attractive sports car that was a classic in its own way: the Lea-Francis. It was built near the Jaguar factory in Coventry, but only in relatively small numbers because it was rather expensive. At first it had a 1.5-litre, or 1.7-litre,

ABOVE *The principle of building a high-performance car using saloon car components was followed by Porsche in the 1950s. Some little marvels like this 1955 Speedster were produced which took their inspiration from Volkswagen. Gradually, Porsche developed its own components, but kept the original VW layout.*
LEFT *The Aston Martin DB2 was an early product of the union between two of Great Britain's most-respected car manufacturers: Aston Martin supplied the chassis and body, and Lagonda provided the 2.6-litre engine that was to power this beautiful car (illustrated in 1952 form) to many competition successes.*

four-cylinder engine designed by Hugh Rose, who had been with Riley before the war. It was beautifully built but rather heavy, and so it was not until a 2.5-litre version of the engine was fitted from 1949 that the Lea-Francis was capable of reaching 160 km/h (100 mph). These engines, and the Lea-Francis's torsion bar independent front suspension, were used with great success in the British Connaught Formula 2 and sports racing cars. (A torsion bar is a rod that absorbs energy by being twisted along its length.) But like Allard, Lea-Francis faced overwhelming competition from Jaguar.

Jaguar's chief opposition in competition came from a variety of cars which are discussed in the last chapter, plus Aston Martins which proved to be just as good on the road. The first postwar Aston Martin, made in 1948, was a beautifully built, but rather heavy, touring car called the DB1. It took its initials from the industrialist David Brown, who had bought the ailing Aston Martin and Lagonda firms in 1947. Like all Aston Martins before it, the DB1 handled superbly with its independent front suspension and well-

located coil-spring rear axle in a rigid tubular chassis. However, the 2-litre four-cylinder pushrod engine was designed more with an eye to economy than high performance, so David Brown decided to replace it with a twin overhead camshaft six-cylinder unit that had been designed for Lagonda's postwar saloons. With this engine installed in a modified version of the DB1's chassis and clothed in a beautiful Italian-inspired GT body, the resultant Aston Martin DB2 was to become one of the greatest of classic sports cars. The cars, from Feltham, Middlesex, were closer in concept to a Ferrari than anything in Britain at the time and, although they lacked the sheer power of the bigger Ferraris, they made up for it with superb handling. They proved to be practical and docile road cars as well. But Aston Martins could not be produced in the same numbers as Jaguars and therefore they remained highly priced.

Jowett, in Bradford, Yorkshire, intended to produce cars in Jaguar quantities, and introduced a sports car of advanced design in 1950 that was also something of a classic: the Jupiter. This had a substantial spaceframe designed by Eberan von Eberhorst, an associate of Professor Porsche, who had worked on the Cisitalia. The Jupiter handled very well and used a flat four-cylinder 1.5-litre engine that was shared with Jowett's successful Javelin saloon and gave the sports car a 135 km/h (85 mph) top speed when equipped with a comfortable touring body, and more than 145 km/h (90 mph) in later tune. Sports racing versions using a skimpy body with wings like cycle mudguards won their class three times at Le Mans from 1950 to 1952.

As a result of demand inspired by competition successes, Porsche was able gradually to increase production of the

The AC Ace, which resembled the Ferrari Barchetta, was developed by John Tojeiro from the successful Cooper-MG sports cars of the early 1950s. His design was taken over by AC, who fitted the Ace with the company's own six-cylinder engine in 1954, before offering more powerful Bristol and Ford units as alternatives.

Type 356 in the early 1950s and, in company with Jaguar, it was soon available in open and closed forms. Porsche spent a great deal of time and effort developing racing cars, with the result that the company's road vehicles, which had to foot the bill, were expensive. One of the most successful racing projects was a four-overhead camshaft flat four-cylinder engine for the Type 550 sports racing car. Almost all major components on a Porsche were interchangeable with those of other models, so these engines soon found their way into road cars. The result was the Porsche Carrera, named after the marque's success in the gruelling Carrera Panamericana road race in Mexico. These rapid little cars were equally at home in competition and on the road and are among the most significant of classic Porsches. Open versions with a minimum of equipment, called Speedsters, were also marketed and soon found a place in Americans' hearts as one of the ultimate 'fun cars', particularly on the West Coast.

Porsches sold well in America alongside medium-priced Jaguar XKs and the rare and expensive exotics such as Ferraris, which are discussed in the penultimate chapter. Most of the market was taken up, however, by the three cheaper British marques: MG which was still producing the glorious T series cars in slightly modernized form, and the new Austin-Healey and Triumph. These simple, powerful, four-cylinder Austin-Healey 100s and Triumph TRs were the first 160 km/h (100 mph) sports cars that almost anybody could afford. They introduced a whole new generation to the delights of open-air motoring.

Apart from firms such as Ferrari, three other

manufacturers made outstanding sports cars in this period: they were Aston Martin, who installed the world's first hatchback door on the lovely DB2/4 coupé in 1953; Alfa Romeo, who brought out the brilliant Giulietta Sprint in 1954; and AC, the tiny British firm from Thames Ditton, Surrey, who put the Tojeiro sports racing car into production in 1954 as the AC Ace.

The Aston Martin DB2/4 was similar to the DB2 except that it was cunningly re-arranged inside to make room for two tiny rear seats, and from late 1954 had a larger 3-litre engine. It was also available in drophead form.

Alfa Romeo's Giulietta was completely new. It used a 1290 cc twin-cam four-cylinder engine in a light unitary-construction body (made in saloon, coupé and two-seater open, or Spider, form), with suspension that ensured excellent handling. (The term Spider dates back to the days when gentlemen raced the lightest possible horse-drawn carriages, whose progress resembled that of a scuttling spider.) The engine was available in varying stages of tune with the best example in the Sprint Speciale producing 100 bhp, which gave 200 km/h (124 mph). This car remains one of the most beautiful coupés ever produced by the Italian firm.

The AC Ace was the first British postwar sports car to use all-independent suspension, by transverse leaf springs and 'wishbones' (transverse links). It was based on the successful sports racing car designed by John Tojeiro, who in turn was inspired by Cooper racing car company's MG- and Bristol-powered cars. The AC Ace had a chassis made of large diameter tubes and was powered initially by AC's own 2-litre six-cylinder engine rather than the 2-litre Bristol engine used in the Tojeiro. The body, which was influenced by the early Ferrari sports cars, was outstandingly good looking and was also available as a coupé called the Aceca. Later examples of these ACs used the more powerful Bristol engine and were capable of 195 km/h (120 mph), as against 170 km/h (105 mph) attainable with the AC unit.

In America, Chevrolet introduced the Corvette in 1953 and Ford produced a 'personal car' called the Thunderbird, which was more like a convertible that a sports car. The Ford was good for 182 km/h (113 mph) with its most powerful option of engine but lacked any other sports car attributes, such as good handling or stopping ability.

The MG company managed to persuade its parent, the British Motor Corporation, to let it replace the T series cars, which had been produced in TD and TF forms, with the new MGA. This all-enveloping sports car had been shelved when the new Austin-Healey was introduced by BMC in 1952. The simple, reliable MGA, powered by a 1.5-litre engine, was not as fast as the Austin-Healey or Triumph TRs but the handling was far better and it became an immediate best-seller. Prototype versions had twin-cam engines and one of these units was developed for the MGA in 1958 in an attempt to put its performance on a par with Porsche's Type 356s, the Triumph TRs, and six-cylinder versions of the Austin-Healey introduced in 1956. The Twin Cam MGA needed specialized maintenance, however, and soon gained a reputation for unreliability. As a result, only 2000 were made against nearly 100,000 MGAs with the more sedate pushrod engines; nevertheless, because of its

high performance, the Twin Cam must be considered the classic MGA. The Austin-Healeys produced in the late 1950s with the six-cylinder engine, rather than the original four-cylinder of the same capacity, did not handle quite so well, so the early cars can be considered the best Austin-Healeys.

Triumph improved its sports cars by fitting disc brakes on the front wheels of the TR3 in 1956, the first mass-produced car to use this advanced form of braking. Jaguar soon followed suit by fitting disc brakes all round to the XK150 in 1957. Meanwhile in the United States, Ford abandoned any claims that the Thunderbird might have been a sports car by turning it into a five-seater convertible, leaving Chevrolet producing the only home-grown American sports car in the Corvette. This model survived disappointing early sales to become established as America's own sports car when it was fitted with fuel injection on its most powerful engine options. Late in 1954 Mercedes produced the 190SL, a superficially similar car to the company's exotic 300SL. The SL designation stood for Super Light and was justified in the case of the 300SL which used a spaceframe. The 190SL, however, was based on the existing 1.9-litre Mercedes 180 saloon car and made use of its floorpan as well as its mechanical components. As a result it was rather heavy and underpowered in comparison to the 300SL, but was beautifully made.

With the sad demise of Cisitalia, Mercedes was the only spaceframed car in regular production in the 1950s until a brilliant engineer called Colin Chapman got to work in a shed in North London. He built half a dozen competition

---

The British Triumph company produced one of the first 160 km/h (100 mph) sports cars that the man in the street could afford, by using parts from its associated company, Standard. These included an engine that in basic form also saw service in a Ferguson tractor! The car shown here is a 1959 TR3A.

The Lotus Mark 6 designed by Colin Chapman in 1952 was
the first of the really high-performance kit cars to be built in
Great Britain. It featured a spaceframe and simple alloy panels that
could be easily assembled by an enthusiastic customer around
a small engine of his own choice.

The Austin-Healey Sprite introduced in 1958 was
a highly successful, cheap and attractive sports car based on
components from the Austin A35 and Morris Minor saloons. Its cheeky
'grinning' radiator grille and 'Frogeye' headlamps appealed to
enthusiasts as much as its economical performance.

cars for equally impecunious friends before solving the problem of lack of the space (and finance) to run a production line by turning his latest design into a kit to take customers' own mechanical components: this was the Lotus Mark 6 of 1952, a very light and spartan spaceframed sports car that could be powered by a variety of small saloon and sports car engines. Highly tuned versions of the MG T series power unit were among the best used. Like all Lotus cars to follow, these machines handled superbly and, because of their extremely low weight, turned in a good performance too.

An engineer has been defined as somebody who can achieve for a few pence what anyone else would do for a pound: on this basis Donald Healey certainly qualified as a brilliant motoring engineer with his 1958 Austin-Healey Sprite. This frugal two-seater used parts from Austin A35 and Morris Minor saloons with a new bodyshell of extreme simplicity. Healey always had original ideas about reducing wind resistance and featured a unique folding windscreen on the first Healey 100, which had been taken over by BMC as the Austin-Healey 100. Now, with the Sprite, he intended to use retractable headlamps. The mechanism needed to raise and lower them from the bonnet top proved to be too expensive, so Healey simply left the lights in cheap pods on top of the bonnet. By a quirk of fate the Sprite's radiator grille had a 'grinning' appearance, which in combination with the headlights perched on top, made the front of the car look like a frog. This squat little sports car was promptly christened the 'Frogeye' Sprite and charmed enthusiasts everywhere. It proved to be extremely durable and economical, and must rate as one of the classic small sports cars.

By the early 1960s, the public's concept of a sports car was changing from that of a cramped, uncomfortable, high-performance vehicle devoid of much weather protection, or with only a vestigial roof tacked on top, into a fully equipped and sophisticated machine intended for covering long distances at high speeds, or at least turning heads when driven through a city. As the image of a sports car 'softened' to nearer that of a Grand Touring car, some manufacturers continued to produce traditional machines with only token attempts at modernization such as winding windows, while others introduced new models.

One of the biggest surprises came from Daimler, whose previous 'sports cars' had been rather opulent open versions of its saloons. The new sports car for 1959 was completely different. It was the Dart, designed by Edward Turner, who had been responsible for the highly successful Triumph twin-cylinder motorcycles. He produced a new V8 engine of only 2.6 litres capacity that bore a distinct resemblance to four Triumph motorcycle engines put together! There was nothing new in this theory. One of the most successful Grand Prix cars of the period, the Vanwall, took the engine of Triumph's rival motorcycle, the single-cylinder Norton, as its inspiration.

The new Daimler's chassis was very similar to that of the Triumph TR3 sports car, but the body was unlike that of any other car except perhaps Citroën's DS saloon, which had a similar nose. This body, which featured a very large luggage boot, making it really unusual among sports cars of the day, was constructed from glass fibre. This kept the Dart's weight down and gave it a 196 km/h (122 mph) top speed with excellent fuel consumption. It was quite a package and sold reasonably well to people who were not put off by its highly individual styling. Naturally this Daimler had a comfortable interior and wind-up windows, as befitted a product from a maker of limousines.

With competition such as this, and the new Sunbeam Alpine from Rootes, who traditionally made slightly more comfortable cars than those of its mass-production rivals, the high-volume classics, like the Austin-Healeys, Triumph TRs and MGs, were made more civilized. In the case of the Big Healey, as it was to become known to distinguish it from the Frogeye, the 3000 Mark III convertible made from 1964 was the most desirable; the TR was restyled as the TR4 in 1961 and could be bought with a Surrey top, a combination of divided hard top and soft top that was adopted later by Porsche; and MG at last produced a unitary-construction sports car in the MGB of 1962. This was to stay in production with little change until 1980 to make it one of the longest-surviving classic sports cars.

In the United States, Corvettes were changed in detail every year, with a substantial restyling as the Sting Ray in 1963. The facelift came just in time because Ford in America introduced the dramatic new Mustang in 1964, which amounted to a four-seater sporting sedan with 180 km/h (110 mph) performance from its most powerful engine option. The concept of half saloon car and half sports car was so successful that the model sold half a million in 18 months.

European sports and GT cars were made in much smaller quantities. Aston Martin was firmly positioned in the exotic car classes with the DB4 in the early 1960s, as Jaguar E type production was limited by the demand for Jaguar saloons. The Swedish manufacturer Volvo joined the sports car market and in 1960 had ambitious plans to produce the P1800S coupé in Scotland – immortalized in *The Saint* series on British TV. These plans did not materialize, however, although the body continued to be made in Britain! Like Volvo's saloons and trucks, this 1.7-litre four-cylinder car was an extremely strong machine and made up for its rather stodgy image by reaching a 180 km/h (110 mph) maximum speed.

The Mercedes 'sports car' was revised as the 230SL in 1963 – like the Ford Mustang, it was very close to a small saloon car in concept. One of the most attractive features of this well-made and expensive car was the pagoda-styled hard top. In 1962 Alfa Romeo, back into stride after recovery from heavy war damage, with large quantities of American Marshall Aid, produced a 1600 cc version of the Giulietta's twin-cam engine for a new range of medium-sized cars called Giulias. This range was as extensive as the smaller Giulietta, and in some cases the larger engine was squeezed into the smaller car to give even better performance. A wide variety of permutations was listed, with the 1600 SS, which was a Giulia version of a Giulietta

Sprint Speciale, and the Giulia GTV as top of the range.

In 1964 the British firm of Rootes built a competition version of its Sunbeam Alpine, the Tiger, with a Ford V8 engine. This car was soon put into production as a mildly modified Sunbeam Alpine with a 4.2-litre Ford engine. The resultant Tiger was an extremely flexible and fast sports car at a modest price. A larger, 4.7-litre version of the Ford Fairlane saloon engine had been shoehorned into one of the tiny Mark III coupés built by TVR at Blackpool in 1963. In its least potent form, this engine produced more than twice the power of the MG and Ford four-cylinder engines that the Mark III had been designed to accommodate, and endowed this TVR with a fearsome performance. These models were known as TVR Griffiths after the American dealer who had commissioned them. With a 195 bhp Fairlane engine they were capable of 225 km/h (140 mph); nearly 275 km/h (170 mph) was possible with a hotter 271 bhp version. Sadly, they did not have the handling to match the potential speed, but they remain the epitome of a classic aggressive sports car.

One of the most stunning sports cars in the world was introduced in 1962 when British racing driver Jem Marsh teamed up with former Lotus aerodynamicist Frank Costin to make Marcos GT cars. After building a few rather weird-looking coupés with gullwing doors that were quite successful in competition, they produced the definitive 1600 coupé, one of the lowest cars ever to go into production. The driver and passenger reclined like the occupants of a racing car; once they were inside the Marcos it was quite comfortable! The performance and handling were excellent with these desirable sports cars (early versions of which had a sturdy wooden chassis) powered by engines varying from a 1.6-litre Ford to a 3-litre Volvo.

Frank Costin's previous employer, Lotus, produced one of its most successful sports cars at this time: the Elan. It replaced the Elite and used a twin-cam version of the Ford Cortina four-cylinder engine, which was also fitted to the Lotus 23B sports racing car and Lotus Cortina saloon. The Lotus Elan, introduced in 1963 in open form, had a backbone chassis with glass-fibre coachwork and handled as well as any other Lotus – in other words, superbly! It still needed dedicated attention, but not quite so much as that required by the Elite. One of its novelties was the use of rubber 'doughnuts' in the drive line to cushion sharp gear changes, which caused novice drivers to make it leap along like a kangaroo as the rubber wound and unwound itself. Other features of this rapid machine included electric

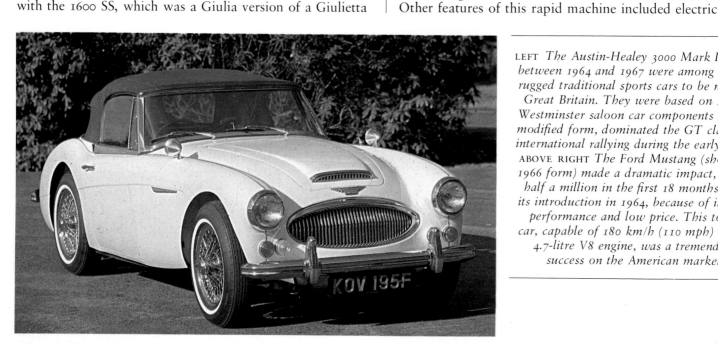

LEFT *The Austin-Healey 3000 Mark IIIs built between 1964 and 1967 were among the last rugged traditional sports cars to be made in Great Britain. They were based on Austin Westminster saloon car components and, in modified form, dominated the GT classes in international rallying during the early 1960s.*
ABOVE RIGHT *The Ford Mustang (shown in 1966 form) made a dramatic impact, selling half a million in the first 18 months after its introduction in 1964, because of its high performance and low price. This tough car, capable of 180 km/h (110 mph) with a 4.7-litre V8 engine, was a tremendous success on the American market.*

window lifts to leave the driver's hands free for more important functions.

In the early 1960s Porsche was working on a replacement for the ageing Type 356 series. Eventually, the company's second great classic GT car, the 911, went into production in 1964. This followed the same basic layout as the four-cylinder Type 356, but had a sleeker body, still mounted on a platform chassis, and used a six-cylinder rear-mounted, air-cooled engine. The handling could be tricky on these early Porsche 911s because of the engine's weight behind the rear axle line, but to have placed the engine ahead of the rear axle, as in racing Porsches, would have left no room in this GT car for the small rear seats Porsche considered to be essential. These beautifully built machines immediately became bestsellers for the German firm and have since been developed through numerous variations, including ultra-lightweight versions for racing, to become one of the all-time classic sports cars.

In America, Chevrolet made a big improvement to the Corvette in 1965 by fitting disc brakes all round. The old drum brakes had worked reasonably well, but the new discs were much better. However, their late adoption emphasized how far American sports-car standards were behind those of Europe. The Corvette continued to change in detail appearance every year until 1969, when it was restyled to great effect along the lines of an earlier Mako Shark show car. Throughout the years of the late 1960s it was always able to hold its own among the American 'muscle' cars, such as the Ford Mustangs and AC Cobras, and the high-powered Plymouths, Oldsmobile 4-4-2s and Pontiac GTOs. These American compact saloons used a variety of large V8 engines but were never quite in the same league as the Corvette Sting Ray with equivalent power.

Fiat also produced a classic sports car in 1967: the Dino. This was basically a neat amalgam of existing Fiat sports and saloon car components forming an open two-seater or, with a special bodyshell, an attractive coupé. The power unit was a production version of Ferrari's 2-litre V6 unit intended for Formula 2 racing. The regulations covering Formula 2 at the time demanded that the engine blocks had to be from production cars, at least 500 of which had been produced and sold. Fiat, which had taken a substantial share in Ferrari, agreed to market the Dino in this form to qualify the Ferrari engine for Formula 2 racing. The result was an excellent sports car.

The Morgan continued substantially unchanged with a variety of Ford or Triumph power units; a few aerodynamic coupés were made but most products of this British company differed little from the prewar four-wheelers. When Triumph decided to discontinue the four-cylinder engine in the TR4A (a TR4 with independent rear suspension), the problem arose of finding a new power unit because the six-cylinder unit that would be fitted to the new TR5 was too long for the Morgan. A Ford V6 engine was tried, but it was found to be too tall and heavy, but then Morgan managed to squeeze in one of the new all-alloy Rover V8 engines. This 3.5-litre unit, based on an engine used in Buicks and Oldsmobiles in the early 1960s, produced abundant power and torque and endowed the new Morgan Plus 8 with a sensational 200 km/h (125 mph) performance. Little else changed on the car, making it a fascinating anachronism.

Among the small British specialist manufacturers, Ginetta produced an attractive little sports car in the mid-1960s called the G4. It featured a spaceframe, coil spring suspension and a glass-fibre body, and used a 997 cc Ford Anglia engine. All manner of tuning equipment was available for this engine and gave the Ginetta an excellent performance: a classic among cars that can be built from kits.

Towards the end of the 1960s, several of the traditional

sports cars had to be redesigned or were discontinued because of stringent American exhaust emission and safety regulations: it was no longer possible to produce sports cars only for the European market because of the low potential sales and high development costs. The Big Healey was one of the cars that had to be abandoned and the Jaguar E type's performance was watered down to around 210 km/h (130 mph) from nearer 240 km/h (150 mph).

The Japanese surveyed this scene carefully and produced the Datsun 240Z, which amounted to a neat combination of the strongest points of the Big Healey and the Jaguar E type fixed-head coupé. The car was built at a very competitive price and swept the American market. However, by 1974 the 240Z had been increased in weight and had begun to depart from the classic sports car image, moving more towards the sporting saloons.

Jaguar restored the performance of its E type by

installing the V12 engine which had been designed for the XJ saloon, rather in the same manner as the company had tried the six-cylinder unit in the XK120 before installing it in the Mark VII saloon more than 20 years earlier. In this case the V12 engine did not make its appearance in a saloon until a year after it had been fitted to the sports car. However, like the Datsun 240Z, these V12 E types were of a softer character than the early machines. Nevertheless they can both be considered classics: the early 3.8-litre E types because of their uncompromising performance and trend-setting appearance, and the later V12 ones because they were some of the last high-performance cheap sports cars.

In 1973 MG, which had long fought a battle with BMC to improve its cars technically or introduce new models, but had been refused on the grounds of cost or of causing potential conflict with rival Triumph models within the same group, at last managed to get a supply of the Rover V8 engines for the MGB GT V8. Despite having what amounted to an antique shell, this wonderfully 'long-legged' cruiser had excellent handling because the engine, although far more powerful than the original four-cylinder unit, weighed no more. It had not been available before because almost every one made was needed for Rover's saloons: the small number supplied to Morgan made little difference,

LEFT *The Morgan Plus 8 introduced in 1968 looked – and felt – almost exactly the same as the first four-wheel Morgan built in 1935! But it went much faster, up to 200 km/h (125 mph), because of its light alloy Rover V8 3.5-litre engine rather than the original, tame four-cylinder unit.*

whereas it was anticipated that an MG V8 would be so popular that the demand would have been greater than BMC's production capacity. However, no sooner had this classic MG been introduced than the world energy crisis occurred, and sales suffered as a result.

MG had produced a number of prototypes which bore a resemblance, by coincidence, to Fiats produced at the same time. One of the last of these experimental cars was a well-designed wedge-shaped coupé that was very much like the Fiat X1/9 of 1972. This charming little Italian car was to sell well into the 1980s as a baby Ferrari in the absence of much competition from other manufacturers. One of the reasons MG had not been allowed to proceed with its new car was that a new Triumph TR was planned, the TR7, which was of fashionable wedge-shaped styling. However, sports car enthusiasts considered the TR7 to be too much like the Triumph Dolomite saloons and sales suffered as a result of this.

In the more expensive class, Mercedes continued to update its sporting SL series along the lines of the saloons, fitting V8 engines to the 350 and 450SL to make them formidable high performers. Various small British manufacturers, notably TVR, continued to produce sports cars. TVR's Turbo model was exceptional. Its turbocharged Ford V6 engine gave it a shattering 225 km/h (140 mph) performance with good handling from a well-developed chassis. (Turbocharging is used to develop more power without increasing the size of the engine. It involves an exhaust driven turbine that forces more mixture into the engine, thus giving increased power.) The Lotus Esprit, based on the 2-litre Elite produced since 1974, has proved to be an exceptionally stylish wedge-shaped sports coupé with handling as good as any previous Lotus. Its performance was also improved when it was turbocharged in 1980.

Sports car sales generally were low, however, as the car industry went into the 1980s. Their popularity had been badly hit in the 1960s and 1970s by the advent of high-performance small saloons such as the Mini-Cooper S and Ford Escorts developed for rallying. These relatively cheap cars offered at least as much performance as a sports car with considerably greater carrying capacity. The result was that effectively they took the place of the sports car and by the 1980s the classic age of the open-topped high performer was at an end.

BELOW *The Datsun 240Z introduced in 1970 was a very popular sports car with its high performance, cheap price and sturdy reliability. Relatively few examples were sold in Europe because most of the production went to the USA where there was a huge demand.*

SALOON CARS AND CONVERTIBLES

ABOVE *The 'Continental' coachwork by Mulliner on a close-coupled Bentley chassis made one of the most desirable cars in the world in 1952. This magnificent limousine could outperform almost every other car on the road, yet carry its passengers in the greatest of comfort.*

RIGHT *The Bristol 400 of 1947, based on a prewar BMW design, was a beautifully built four-seater sporting saloon that had an excellent performance from only 2 litres. It was capable of 151 km/h (94 mph) with first-class acceleration, economy and handling: a real classic.*

Car manufacturers everywhere concentrated on making saloons with a few convertible equivalents as soon as the Second World War was over. It was what the motoring public needed and wanted most; but few of these cars could be considered classics. Most of them were mundane because the priority was actually producing a car, any car, in the face of crippling shortages of raw materials and car components. For simplicity, nearly all the saloon cars were based on prewar designs; and the convertibles were just saloon cars with the tops lopped off, sometimes quite crudely.

Even the Americans had some problems, despite having had two more years for development before the war engulfed them in 1941. Automatic transmissions had already started to appear on American saloon cars, but these hardly made them classics because of their inefficiency. The best that could be said about American cars of this period is that they had some nostalgic titbits. The wood-clad bodies on the Chrysler Town and Country cars made between 1946 and 1948 were rather glorious. But they did not last long as every piece of maple trim had to be fashioned from a solid block. And the nine 'teeth' on the front of a 1950 Buick were in classical bad taste! Most of the styling in America in this early postwar period followed trends set by Studebaker.

A number of good cars could be found in Europe, however, even if the average customer faced a waiting list of up to seven years. The world's fastest production saloon car at the time, the Healey Elliot, was a British example. This saloon, with its Westland convertible equivalent, was designed while Donald Healey and his friends, Sammy Sampietro and Ken Bowden, were working on Humber armoured cars during the war. The box-section chassis followed conventional lines with Volkswagen-inspired independent front suspension and Riley running gear, including the 2.5-litre four-cylinder engine. Sheet steel was in very short supply, so an attractive alloy body was built on a wooden frame. These cars, produced in a corner of a concrete-mixer factory in Warwick, promptly cleared 167 km/h (104 mph) in 1946.

Sydney Allard produced saloon versions of his sports and touring cars but they were very heavy and were not as fast as the lightweight Healey. Riley also made its own 1.5-litre and 2.5-litre saloons, the RM series, in the MG works at Abingdon but, like the Allards, they were heavy and slower than the Healey. They were of an endearingly elegant prewar design, however, and are classics in their own right, with a rare three-seater 2.5-litre tourer as the most desirable. MG produced a saloon and tourer at the same time based on the contemporary Morris Ten. This was the Y type, which had been designed before the war and used a similar engine to that of the MG TC sports car. Its chassis was more advanced, however: it used independent front suspension and eventually formed the basis of the TC's successor, the TD, in 1949. Like the Rileys, these prewar style MGs were delightful cars, even if rather sedate. The Jaguar saloons built in this era were larger, but were laid out along similar lines to the Riley and the MG.

Bristol relied heavily on the prewar BMW 327 for inspiration for its expensive saloons as the company had

An extraordinary American classic was the Chrysler Town and Country 'Woodie' made in various guises immediately after the Second World War. Its half-timbered body was described as having 'the grace and elegance of a yacht'. Unfortunately, the handling on this stylish convertible left a lot to be desired.

taken over the German firm's designs as war reparations. The first automotive products of this British aircraft manufacturer, the 400 series built in 1947, stayed close to the BMW specifications with a six-cylinder overhead-valve pushrod engine, independent front suspension, and rack and pinion steering. The body, which also closely resembled a BMW, was of exceptionally low drag and gave the 400 a top speed of 151 km/h (94 mph).

The French produced two significant saloon cars during this period and both came from Citroën. It would be logical to assume that there would be a close resemblance, but the French have long produced cars that owe nothing to preconceived notions. The Citroën *traction-avant* and the 2CV both had front-wheel drive and unitary construction, but that was where the resemblance ended. The larger *traction-avant* had a 140 km/h (85 mph) performance in its most powerful form, with excellent handling and styling that dated back to 1934 (the year of its introduction). This was the car that was immortalized by the British television series *Maigret* about the French detective. The other Citroën, the *deux chevaux*, or 2CV, started life in 1949 as an incredibly economical 375 cc mobile garden shed; its body looked just like that and it went about as slowly as you would expect. However, the simplicity and ease of maintenance certainly paid dividends as variants of the 2CV were still in production in the 1980s. This was to be the car that virtually put France on wheels, with its very flexible coil spring suspension absorbing ridges and potholes on back roads with no trouble at all.

Even the proud names of Rolls-Royce and Bentley had to think in terms of less costly cars after the war. Rolls dropped its glorious V12 Phantom III and introduced the six-cylinder Silver Wraith model in 1947 because there was not sufficient demand for bespoke coachwork to take up all the chassis the works could make. Therefore Rolls started building the Silver Dawn with a standardized factory body in 1949. This used the same panels as the Bentley Mark VI which had been in production since 1946. Various coach-

built Rolls continued to be produced in small quantities, including the straight eight-cylinder Phantom IVs for heads of state and royalty, but by 1951 the normal Rolls and Bentley products were distinguishable only by their different radiators and badges (Rolls-Royce had taken over Bentley in 1931). They were still magnificent vehicles, however, and few people disputed Rolls-Royce's claim to be the best car in the world. Soon after, in 1952, Mulliner introduced its special two-door fastback 'Continental' coachwork on the Bentley chassis to produce one of the most remarkable saloon cars ever. The highly geared Bentley Continental was capable of cruising with great silence and dignity at more than 160 km/h (100 mph) with a maximum speed of 190 km/h (120 mph) and, because of its relatively low weight, it also handled well. In addition it provided a degree of comfort difficult to equal elsewhere. These were incomparable cars at an almost incomparable price – around £7000 in Britain in 1952.

Meanwhile Jaguar was hard at work designing a new saloon car. The company followed the time-honoured practice, which was especially prevalent in America, of not introducing a completely new car, but changing its models in stages: the body one year, the chassis another, and then the engine. Thus it might appear that new models were being brought out at reasonably short intervals, when in fact only a part of them was actually new. This meant that at any one time a Jaguar was principally made up of well-

RIGHT *This 1952 Rolls-Royce Silver Wraith has coachwork by Hooper that followed the lines of the standard car, but was lavish, to say the least, in its appointments.*
BELOW *The Citroën 2CV could only have been made in France such was its originality of design. It featured a tiny air-cooled engine for economy because of the high price of fuel in France, and very flexible suspension to cope with rough roads and farm tracks.*

tried components and there was longer to develop new ones. This was especially important with the postwar trend towards new all-enveloping bodies, which took much longer to prepare for production because they needed complicated new tools and presses for their large panels. It was much quicker to introduce a new body built up from small bits and pieces in the traditional manner, but far less efficient.

All the above factors influenced the introduction of the Mark V Jaguar in 1948. In many ways the Jaguars produced immediately after the war were very much like the prewar Bentleys, except that they were far cheaper. Bentley went over to independent front suspension with its short-lived Mark V model in 1940 as Jaguar was experimenting with this advanced new form of suspension. The system Jaguar eventually perfected was inspired by the Citroën *traction-avant*'s torsion bar and wishbone layout, except that it used a brilliantly simple independent front suspension linkage designed by chief engineer William Heynes. A new chassis was designed specially to take this independent front suspension and provide greater rigidity at the same time. The existing 2.5-litre and 3.5-litre engines that had been Jaguar's mainstay since 1938 were fitted into this new chassis with an interim body built up from small parts in the Jaguar factory. The rival Bentley had been redesigned in 1946 and named the Mark VI; so this Jaguar was designated the Mark V and the new 1952 model, complete with new body and new engine, was called the Mark VII! The XK engine used in the Mark VII had already been tested in the XK120 sports car, which used a shortened version of the Mark V chassis. With the competition successes

of the XK120 and its special racing versions, orders poured in for the new Mark VII, whose body had benefited from the years spent preparing presses and tools to make it. Nevertheless, the interim Mark V car was also an attractive machine and deserves classic status as the best of the early Jaguar saloons.

Jowett made use of torsion-bar suspension all round on its new Javelin saloon car in 1947. The firm recognized this system as an efficient space saver and found a flat four-cylinder engine attractive for the same reason – and practical because its cars always had power units of such a configuration. However, detail engineering on this new unit was to let Jowett down. The Javelin, of unitary construction, unlike the spaceframed Jupiter sports car, which used the same engine, was a beautifully designed six-seater with a top speed of 130 km/h (80 mph). Sadly, demand fell off for these thoroughly modern classics which suffered so much from teething troubles that were not cured until 1953. The body pressings were too complicated to produce in the parent factory, so Jowett had to rely on an outside contractor. When the company could not sell enough cars to keep up with the contractor's production capacity, Ford filled the gap at the body works and Jowett's supplies ended. It took a brave firm to plunge headlong into modern design and production methods after the war.

As a result, most of the classic saloon cars came from relatively small manufacturers. Bristol was backed by an aircraft giant but produced only a few of its prestige saloons. The company rebodied the 400 in 1949 but changed little else. This new car, whose body was developed in the parent company's wind tunnel and by testing along a two-mile runway built for the giant Brabazon aircraft, was designated the 401. Its aerodynamics were so good that few cars produced since have had a lower drag coefficient – or a more aerodynamic shape to put it another way. As a result, this well-equipped sports saloon was capable of 172 km/h (107 mph) with a fuel consumption that was better than 14 litres/100 km (20 mpg). A few 402 model convertibles which suffered from a body that was not sufficiently rigid were built before the type 403 was introduced in 1953. Detail improvements were made to the suspension and gearchange and more powerful engine options listed to make this one of the most desirable early Bristols.

The Lagondas that had been designed by W.O. Bentley (whose own firm had been bought by Rolls-Royce in 1931) were produced in equally small numbers. They benefited from having a gearbox made by Lagonda's parent company, David Brown, rather than a complicated Cotal gearbox with an electrically operated gear change, but apart from that they were substantially unchanged from the design W.O. Bentley had wanted to put into production in 1945. David Brown eventually produced these sumptuous, all-independently sprung saloons alongside his Aston Martin sports cars and introduced a drophead version in 1951. These heavy, expensive, sporting vehicles sold reasonably well until 1956, when costs became too high.

W.O. Bentley chose not to join David Brown when that company absorbed Lagonda in 1947, and went to work as a consultant for Armstrong Siddeley, whose parent company, Hawker Siddeley, like Bristol, was an aircraft manufacturer. Armstrong Siddeleys had gained a reputation for being rather stodgy saloons but they were no mean performers in the immediate postwar years. In 1953, a modern 3.4-litre engine with hemispherical combustion chambers was produced and this went into the new Sapphire saloon. This elegant car was slightly more compact than a Jaguar Mark VII and could nearly rival its performance. It suffered badly from competition from the Jaguar, however, and also from the cheaper Rover saloons.

The Rovers produced immediately after the war were almost exactly the same as the prewar cars, but unlike the similarly repetitive MG TC, for instance, they were rather dull. The firm's attention was chiefly occupied with the new Land-Rover utility vehicle up to 1948, with the result that car design took second place. But its first new postwar vehicle, the Rover 75 of 1949, looked completely different from any Rover that had preceded it. It had slab sides, seated six in comfort, and had a very attractive Cyclops-style built-in central foglight. The mechanical side of the car was substantially unaltered but the restyling was so dramatic for such a conservative company that many dyed-in-the-wool Rover buyers were alarmed. However, the car was just as well built as ever and once they had recovered from the shock of realizing that some things in life just have to change they bought every car that the Solihull works could turn out. Various engine options were offered between 2.1 and 2.6 litres, with the original Cyclops 75 and the later high-performance 105S the best of these early saloons, called 'Aunties' by all and sundry.

If the dignified Rover saloon was ideal for Aunt Mildred or the bank manager, the larger Daimlers produced after the war were definitely for dowagers. These limousines, some of which had bespoke coachwork, stuck to the fluid flywheel transmission pioneered by Daimler in 1930. The best of these cars was the DB18, but today they all represent excellent value as classic cars without the reputation of high cost like their Rolls-Royce equivalents.

In the smaller classes the Sunbeam-Talbot 90 of 1948 was an absolute gem. It owed much of its mechanical heritage

to sister saloons made by the Rootes Group in Coventry, but its body was beautiful and the whole car was much improved when it was revised with independent front suspension in 1950. These cars had been sold in France as simply Sunbeams to avoid confusion with the locally made Talbots but, when a roadster version of the 90 was produced in 1953, it, too, was called a Sunbeam rather than a Sunbeam-Talbot. In 1955, the saloon followed suit.

That year also saw the introduction of one of the most significant cars ever made by Jaguar: the Mark I saloon. This was the company's first unitary-construction car and weighed little more than the established XK sports car, despite being a four-to-five seater. Initially it was powered by a short-stroke 2.4-litre version of the XK engine, but later examples, built from 1957, were available with the existing 3.4-litre unit. The performance of both cars was so high, more than 160 km/h (100 mph), and the price so low, that there was nothing else in the same class. The 3.4-litre could reach 195 km/h (120 mph) and, soon after its introduction, was fitted with disc brakes all round as a result. Everything was good about these classic Jaguar saloons: performance, quality, handling, appearance. The larger Jaguar saloons continued to be developed during this period, culminating in the Mark IX of 1958 with its 3.8-litre XK engine and four-wheel disc brakes. The Mark I really filled the gap, however, between the XK sports cars and the big Mark VII, VIII and IX saloons.

The limousine version of the Daimler DB18 made immediately after the Second World War was typical of the carriages used by royalty and heads of state at that time. It was very large with deep windows and an opening rear section, so that the dignitaries could be seen easily by the watching crowds.

Meanwhile, Bristol produced two true classics, the 404 in 1953 and the 405 in 1954. The 404 was an outstandingly good-looking machine with a short wheelbase and two-plus-two seating configuration, and other outstanding qualities that really place it among the exotic cars. The 405 was the only four-door saloon car made by Bristol. It had excellent brakes and handled superbly with a high performance of up to 195 km/h (120 mph) provided by engines in varying degrees of tune. But the most significant feature of the 405 was its styling. In company with the 404, it had tiny rear fins which echoed the large stabilizers on the Type 450 racing Bristol saloons that finished seventh, eighth and ninth and won their class in 1954 and 1955 in the Le Mans 24-hour endurance race. These fins were trend-setters, and the 405 also had a very large expanse of glass, more in keeping with a saloon car of the 1970s than the 1950s. The seating arrangements, too, were well ahead of their time in that the rear seats were contoured like those in the front, making this car a four-seater, rather than a conventional four-to-five seater with a bench-type back seat. Passengers in the back travelled in comfort in this, the best of the early Bristols.

These high standards of design, engineering and construction were shared by Mercedes-Benz in Germany. The first cars made by the Stuttgart firm after the war were based on prewar designs, but the 300 introduced in 1951 was full of new features, even if it still bore a strong family resemblance to earlier cars. This beautifully made four- to five-seater was capable of 155 km/h (95 mph), despite weighing around 1780 kg (3920 lb) because of the efficiency of its 3-litre engine. The swing-axle independent rear suspension could be stiffened to cope with heavy loads by a push button on the dashboard. This button worked an electric motor which operated a torsion bar to supplement the main coil springs. Other ingenious devices included forced-air demisting of the side windows. A four-door

*The 1960 Armstrong-Siddeley Star Sapphire illustrated
here was the last of a long line of British classic cars from a
Coventry firm renowned for producing solidly built vehicles with
good workmanship, comfort and ease of driving. Unlike some previous
Armstrong-Siddeleys it also had an exceptionally good performance
because of its hemispherical head 4-litre engine.*

convertible version of the 300 was also marketed from 1955, with fuel injection and automatic transmission.

Manual gearchanges on saloon cars had virtually disappeared in the United States by 1955 as the American car industry maintained its technological lead in the development of automatic transmission. Rolls-Royce and Bentley followed this trend, fitting a General Motors-based automatic transmission to their new Silver Cloud and S1 models in 1955. These cars had a larger (4.9-litre) six-cylinder engine stretched to the limit of its capacity, and exceptionally elegant steel bodies as standard, although special coachwork could still be ordered on the bare chassis. American-inspired options included air conditioning and power-assisted steering.

The Coventry firm of Alvis had started making Rolls-Royce aero engines during the Second World War and continued building these power units afterwards to such an extent that there was little capacity for car production.

However, Alvis did make small numbers of rather conservative, but very attractive, sports saloons. The company's first entirely new postwar car was the TA21 introduced in 1950. This had a six-cylinder, 3-litre engine and excellent performance. Alec Issigonis (during a brief spell away from Morris) designed an advanced V8-engined saloon for Alvis which, sadly, did not go into production – but a new body did. This was designed by Graber and remains one of the most beautiful saloon cars ever made.

Eventually, Armstrong Siddeley followed Rolls-Royce's lead by introducing the Star Sapphire in 1960 with a larger, 4-litre, engine and automatic transmission as standard. This car had a similar performance to a Rolls-Royce (but was slightly slower than one of the large Jaguars) and was also available in limousine form.

Even Daimler capitulated and offered automatic transmission as an option to its traditional fluid flywheel from 1956, and standardized it on the new 3.8-litre six-

power and torque for its cars and wanting automatic transmission like its rivals, decided to fit a V8. The company had developed a new twin overhead camshaft engine rather like Jaguar's, and was working on a new automatic gearbox when development had to stop because of demands by the aircraft side of the business. In 1961 a Chrysler V8 engine and transmission was fitted to the Bristol 406 to turn it into the 407. The performance was exceptional with a top speed of 200 km/h (125 mph).

At the same time, Daimler was busy further increasing the performance of its big saloon by fitting its own 4.6-litre V8 engine in 1960. This huge car, called the Majestic Major, was extraordinarily fast, reaching 196 km/h (122 mph) with acceleration that left all but the quickest sports cars standing. There simply was nothing else like it in the same class, but production was limited by the fact that Jaguar had bought Daimler in 1960 and needed much of the factory space to produce its own cars. Demand was very high for the Mark II Jaguar saloon; but by 1961 the Mark IX Jaguar was becoming very dated. As a result, Jaguar introduced its biggest saloon ever, the Mark X, which was even wider than a Rolls-Royce Silver Cloud. This enormous car was of unitary construction but still weighed nearly two tons ready for the road, so it was fitted with the high-performance E type sports car engine to retain sufficient speed and acceleration. Because of its sheer size, the Mark X offered exceptionally comfortable interior accommodation which was further heightened by the use of independent rear suspension similar to the E type.

During the late 1950s, Lancia maintained its reputation for producing technically advanced cars with the large 2.5-litre Flaminia saloon of similar design to the Aurelia; the company followed this up with a revolutionary small saloon, the Flavia, in 1961. This had front-wheel drive, a flat four-cylinder engine and disc brakes. Various Italian coachbuilders offered special bodywork on the Lancia platform: designs by Zagato were among the most striking. During this period, Alfa Romeo also produced saloon car equivalents of the Giulietta and Giulia sports cars that were not quite so attractive but offered exceptionally good performance coupled with excellent roadholding.

In the early 1960s the specifications of new classic saloon cars verged on the exotic: Lagonda's Rapide built between 1961 and 1964 was really a stretched, four-door version of the Aston Martin DB4 except that it had de Dion rear suspension and a 4-litre engine rather than the Aston's 3.7 litres; this engine was later to be used in the Aston Martin DB5. The Rapide was a very high performance saloon, being capable of around 225 km/h (140 mph) with even better roadholding than that of the near-legendary DB4 because it had a longer wheelbase. The only drawback, apart from a demanding and expensive maintenance schedule typical of exotic cars, was the rear suspension which lacked development.

In Italy in 1963 Maserati produced an incredible car to a similar concept called the Quattroporte. It had four doors like the Rapide, and a five-speed ZF gearbox and de Dion rear suspension with styling that was spectacular if not quite so good looking. (In the de Dion system the two wheel hubs are attached to the ends of an axle beam but the differential and the exposed drive to the wheels are mounted separately.) Initially this Italian wonder was fitted with a 4.2-litre V8 engine (after the first prototype with a 4-litre unit), which put it in the 210 km/h (130 mph) class. The engine was uprated to 4.7 litres in 1965 and the rear suspension, which proved costly to produce, was changed in favour of a 'live' axle (a single unit enclosed in a rigid housing) used on other Maseratis at the time. Despite its relatively small size, one of these, the two-door Mexico,

cylinder Majestic in 1958. This spectacular saloon could seat six people in great comfort with an unusual amount of leg room in the back, ideal for a limousine in fact. However, its performance was far from sedate: it could top 160 km/h (100 mph) easily and had superb acceleration. What is more, it handled like a sports car and stopped like one, too, with its four-wheel disc brakes. Small wonder that the Daimler Majestic was an instant success.

Trend-setting American saloons during this period included the Cadillac Eldorado Brougham, which was the first car to have air suspension as standard. The company also pioneered the four-headlight system, like Lincoln, in 1957. Cadillac had used tail fins of one sort of another since the fastback of 1948, but these styling gimmicks reached their most extreme form with the Sedan de Ville in 1959. This car is an excellent reflection of American design during that period.

Back in Great Britain, Bristol restyled its cars along more conventional lines, abandoning the fins and reverting to two doors with the 406 of 1958. This car also had a 2.2-litre engine, which gave extra torque (the usable power available at the crankshaft) and made it more relaxing to drive. It was a much bigger car than the earlier Bristols and aimed at taking a share of the Bentley market. In response, Rolls and Bentley produced a new V8 engine for the S series cars in 1960 for the same reason that Bristol had increased the capacity of its engine. Then Bristol, needing more qualified as a saloon car rather than a GT because it had four full-sized seats. Although the Mexico, introduced in 1966, did not look quite like a Quattroporte, it was in effect a two-door version of it.

Mercedes-Benz in Germany produced a giant of a car in 1964, called the 600, or Grosser Mercedes. This huge machine had a 6.3-litre engine and was available in two lengths, with wheelbases of 3.2 m (10 ft 6 in) and 3.9 m (12 ft 10 in). In its longer form, it could be ordered with six doors and measured more than 6.1 m (20 ft)! This impressive limousine proved to be a powerful competitor for Rolls-Royce among heads of states and ambassadors.

Rolls continued to produce its limousine, the Phantom V, with Mulliner, Park Ward coachwork and restyled its Series II saloon with a four-headlight system in 1962. Many of these lovely traditional Rolls and Bentley saloons were fitted with Mulliner, Park Ward coachwork in two-door drophead or fixed-head coupé form.

In 1963 Jaguar decided to ring the changes on engines, transmissions, suspensions and bodyshells to increase its range even further. First the company installed the 2.6-litre V8 engine from the Daimler Dart sports car into the Jaguar Mark II bodyshell to produce the Daimler 2.5-litre saloon. Most of these cars were fitted with automatic transmission to make outstandingly smooth-running and relaxing cars. However, the most significant fact about these saloons is that they handled so well because the all-alloy engine was much lighter than Jaguar's XK unit, which had a cast-iron cylinder block.

Later in the year, Jaguar effectively combined the independent rear suspension from the E type and Mark X with a Mark II bodyshell to form the S type, a luxurious compact saloon available with either the 3.4-litre or 3.8-litre XK engine. These were heavier and rode more softly than the sporting Mark II saloons and had the advantage of a restyled rear end, giving a larger luggage boot. Three years later the front was restyled too, and a 4.2-litre engine fitted as standard to make the Jaguar 420, which was also available in Daimler Sovereign guise with different badges and radiator grille. Heavy as they were, these Jaguars and Daimlers made superb fast touring cars, and the Mark X stayed in production as the 420G with the 4.2-litre E type engine which had been fitted since 1965. Two years later, in 1967, Jaguar was taken over by the British Motor Corporation and the Mark II and small Daimler saloon were revised for their final production run of two years in economy form. These cars were named the Jaguar 240 and 340 when fitted with 2.4-litre or 3.4-litre XK engines, or the Daimler V8-250 with the small V8. They represented outstanding value at the time, although items such as leather upholstery, which had been standard, were now optional extras.

Many of Jaguar's developments over the years were incorporated in the sensational new XJ6 introduced in 1968. The rear suspension, engine and transmission were similar to those in the 420; but the bodyshell was completely new and owed a lot to the 420G in dimensions, although it was not quite so big. Jaguar took pains to perfect the handling and overcome problems with noise and vibration that would have been acceptable to many other manufacturers.

The Maserati Quattroporte built in 1963 was, in effect, an exotic Grand Touring car with sumptuous four-door coachwork, rather than the normal short-wheelbase two-door body used for other Maseratis. Despite its bulk, this extraordinary roadburner was capable of more than 210 km/h (130 mph).

*The ultra-lightweight BMW 3.0CSL produced in 1973
was a particularly exciting product of the Bavarian motor works.
With striking styling, many light-alloy panels, sparse trim and the
most powerful of the firm's highly refined straight six-cylinder
engines, it had a top speed of more than 225 km/h (140 mph).*

The result was a 200 km/h (125 mph) five-seater saloon (in 4.2-litre form) that handled better than any other car in the world and cruised as silently as a Rolls-Royce. It was also available with a 2.8-litre XK engine to keep within economical taxation classes in Europe, but was at its best with the well-tried 4.2-litre engine and automatic gearbox.

Rolls-Royce's first unitary-construction car, the Silver Shadow (or T series), was introduced in 1965, with its Bentley equivalent. These beautifully built cars used the existing 6.2-litre V8 engine and transmission and were available in coachbuilt two-door and convertible form. A long-wheelbase version was introduced in 1969 with the engine capacity increased to 6.7 litres. The traditional Phantom V limousine (and later the Phantom VI) continued to be made in small numbers. These cars dominated their class, with only Jaguar and Mercedes able to beat them in any basic terms, such as handling and performance. The Rolls suspension had been intended to work with cross-ply tyres whereas Jaguar's XJ6 had been designed for use with radial-ply tyres from the start and therefore handled better. Rolls-Royce survived bankruptcy (the company's car-manufacturing division was still making a profit) in 1971 to produce the magnificent Corniche drophead or fixed-head coupé. This high-performance two-door limousine with coachwork by Mulliner, Park Ward immediately became the status symbol for the wealthy.

Throughout these years, Mercedes had not been dormant, of course. This Stuttgart firm revised its range early in 1968 with a handsome new body and new independent rear suspension. The most spectacular model became the 300SEL, which used the existing top-of-the-range 300 body with the 600's massive V8 engine. All the luxury items, such as air conditioning, were standard and this classic Mercedes could still manage 220 km/h (137 mph) with outstanding acceleration. The Mercedes range was further refined to introduce a new series in 1971 with the 300SEL in 3.5-litre twin overhead camshaft V8 form.

Mercedes' – and Jaguar's – rival, BMW, had recovered from the devastation of war, and from finding its factories in different halves of a divided Germany, followed by years of financial strain, to produce an excellent coupé in 1968. This was the two-door, four-seater, 2.8-litre 2800CS, which had a 3-litre engine installed in 1971 and reached its ultimate form in the 3.0CSL (3-litre lightweight coupé) in 1973. These were excellent high-speed cruisers with a distinctively sporting appeal after successes on the track.

In 1958 another German manufacturer, NSU, had started making cars, after manufacturing only motorcycles since 1931. These new cars included the world's first Wankel-engined model. This rotating combustion unit developed 50 bhp and was used in NSU's Spyder sports car but the saloon car that followed was far more important. The Ro80 of 1968 was as advanced technologically as the Citroën DS had been in 1955. Its engine had an assessed capacity of 2 litres and it was fitted with a three-speed semi-automatic transmission, all-independent coil-spring suspension and disc brakes all round. The aerodynamics were excellent and the steering impeccable; the only problem with the Ro80 was that the engine needed expensive rebuilds fairly frequently. Nevertheless, this car can still be considered a classic as it

set new standards among saloons, especially its steering.

Bristol continued to develop the 407 during the 1960s through the similar 408 and 409 models to the 410, which was the company's next landmark in 1966. This had 15-inch wheels instead of 16-inch, allowing a wider choice of tyres with the result that it handled better. It had also been restyled in detail with extra chrome, which disappeared with the introduction of the 411 in 1969. This had a far more powerful 6.2-litre Chrysler engine, which gave it a top speed of 225 km/h (140 mph), with roadholding further improved by radial-ply tyres. The 411 received self-levelling suspension the next year in its series II guise, and was revised yet again in 1972 with an impressive four-headlamp system as the 411 series III.

Styling gimmicks aside, American saloon cars, or sedans, had tended to be far more conventional with nothing really classic about them, until Oldsmobile introduced the Toronado in 1965. This massive front-wheel-drive coupé was invariably powered by Oldsmobile's largest engine, which gave it a first class performance with good handling. This configuration was also used on the Cadillac Eldorado Brougham produced by the same parent organization, General Motors.

Jaguar originally designed the XJ6 for a new 5.3-litre 12-cylinder engine which took about 15 years to develop. It was tried first in the E type sports car and eventually went into the XJ saloon in 1972. The results were fantastic, with a 225 km/h (140 mph) maximum speed and handling to match. The only penalty with this machine was that it consumed petrol at the rate of 26 litres/100 km (11 mpg), but this seemed of little importance during the affluent start to the 1970s.

Then the world's energy crisis struck in 1973 and put a whole new complexion on what was desirable in a car. Lotus was one of the first manufacturers to produce a classical economy car, the brilliant Elite, in 1974. This futuristic car, with wedge-shaped styling emulating

ABOVE *Cadillacs have always been among the most impressive American cars, especially the Eldorado convertible. It had everything the average American dreamed of: gadgets galore and engine options up to 8.2 litres. Sadly the convertible was discontinued after threatened changes in safety regulations in 1974.*
RIGHT *The Jaguar XJ12 introduced in 1972 was probably the best saloon car in the world in the 1970s, offering outstanding performance with exceptionally good roadholding, handling, ride and comfort. Like all Jaguars, the XJ12, shown here in Series Two 1974 form, sold at a relatively low price.*

contemporary trends among Grand Prix cars (of which Lotus's were the best), would give around 13 litres/100 km (22 mpg) and up to 210 km/h (130 mph) with a 2-litre engine, while providing seating in great comfort for four people. Handling was in the Grand Prix class, as would be expected from Lotus, and only problems with quality control detracted from the package. They have since been cured and this extraordinary saloon, and the coupé sisters derived from it, fully justify the status of classics.

Alfa Romeo completely revised its range just before the energy crisis in what was to be a far-sighted manner. The Italian company produced two outstanding new saloons, in the 145 km/h (90 mph) Alfasud, with a 1200 cc flat four-cylinder twin overhead camshaft engine, front-wheel drive, and disc brakes all round; and the Alfetta, a larger 164 km/h (112 mph) saloon. The Alfasud's best feature was its handling, which was superb; the rear-wheel-drive Alfetta equalled this by courtesy of de Dion rear suspension. Mercedes went the other way, bringing back the big engine at the top end of the range in the 450SEL 6.9. Since then there have been numerous new saloons, but none could be said to be so far ahead of its contemporaries as to be considered a genuine classic, with the exception of some of the exotic cars described in the next chapter.

EXOTIC CARS

ABOVE *The 1968 Ferrari 365 GTB four-cam, called the Daytona by almost everyone except Enzo Ferrari, was the final embodiment of the front-engined Berlinetta theme. Now a much sought-after classic, it was capable of 278 km/h (174 mph) with astonishing acceleration and superb handling.*

RIGHT *The Lagonda four-door saloon first produced by Aston Martin in 1976 was noted for its excellent engineering, coupled with attractive and distinctive styling by William Towns. Development problems, particularly with its advanced electronic instrument display, delayed substantial production until 1979.*

Exotic cars are machines of outstanding beauty and mechanical refinement built with little regard to cost or economy, and their history since the Second World War is dominated by two Italian marques: Ferrari and Maserati. Maserati was first on the scene with a road car in 1946 while Ferrari was still concentrating on competition machines. However, from 1950, when Ferrari started making touring as well as competition cars, the company's products have been objects of desire, raising the pulses of millions of enthusiasts. This was chiefly because the unique scream of their engines (usually V12s) was so redolent of racing practice.

However, this is not to say that Ferrari has always been ahead of its rivals: far from it, the firm has always been content to let other manufacturers break new ground, relying more on traditional craftsmanship and racing knowledge than inventive genius to gain the desired results. As other marques have come and gone, Ferrari seems set to go on for ever as makers of exotic machinery; and Maserati survives seemingly countless financial crises, each one looking as though it will finish the famous name once and for all. Only Porsche and Aston Martin can equal Ferrari's postwar record for longevity, and the early Porsches and Aston Martins were really sports cars rather than true devil-may-care, hedonistic exotica.

The heart of any Ferrari has always been its engine. These units have invariably made such a glorious howl, and had such animal responsiveness, that almost anything else paled into insignificance beside them. Minor defects, such as a weak clutch and final drive, troublesome electrics or a gigantic turning circle, were disregarded by owners overjoyed by such marvellous machinery under the bonnet. At first this was all Enzo Ferrari and his engineers were really interested in. They certainly did not have time to delve too deeply into bodywork design, leaving that for others to build. All manner of coachbuilders were involved and, in their desperate anxiety not to be seen to be copying each other, many of their results were ghastly. And just as many were built with the Italian climate more in mind than, say, the North American. What matter if the wind and the rain whistled through every nook and cranny? The sound would be drowned by the whoop of that wonderful engine. Nevertheless, some bodies were good and the best often came from Touring and Pinin Farina. In these early days, Ferrari concentrated on competition cars, making only the occasional touring car for a favoured customer.

The first of these was the Type 166 Inter of 1950. This was a slightly detuned and longer wheelbase version of the ferocious 2-litre Mille Miglia, named after Ferrari's victory in that great road race in 1948. It had a five-speed gearbox, leaf spring suspension, tubular chassis and a weak back axle. This was because Ferrari had to use modified Fiat components, like Cisitalia; but subject to more stress because the engines have always produced a lot of power. Ferrari could not afford to make components such as the back axle itself, although the touring cars cost a fortune. All the money the company made went into the development of engines and competition cars generally.

Maserati's road cars have always been a world apart from the racing machines. The straight six-cylinder 1500 cc engine fitted to the Pinin Farina coupés made between 1946 and 1950 was relatively dull compared to the V12s used by Ferrari. But the Maserati factory made more of its own parts in those days, and the 60 or so cars built on an oval tube frame in the immediate postwar years gained a reputation for reliability, despite the fact that the needs of a racing team took priority.

The Pegaso cars built in Barcelona were far more exotic

than either of the Italian products. The chief engineer of this Spanish truck and bus firm, Wilfredo Ricart, who had worked alongside Enzo Ferrari (and Alberto Massimino of Maserati) at Alfa Romeo before the war, decided that he would show the Italians a thing or two. So he sold the idea to Pegaso of building an exotic car to show off Spanish technology to a doubting world. At the same time it would

The Spanish Pegaso remains one of the most exotic cars ever
built. It was what amounted to a roadgoing Grand Prix car with,
in this 1953 model named the Z102B, a 3.2-litre all-alloy twin
overhead camshaft V8 engine, quadruple twin-choke carburettors, five-
speed transaxle, de Dion rear suspension and coachwork by Touring.

provide a goal for the best young engineers on the staff –
far better to be able to say that you had built the most
beautiful car in the world than just a rather splendid bus.
The fantastic result was a Grand Prix car for the road
clothed in bodywork by Pegaso, or by the best of bespoke
coachbuilders such as Touring. The engine was in the
Ferrari class, an all-alloy twin overhead camshaft V8 using
up to four carburettors, with or without supercharger. The
rest of the specification was in a different world, too, with a
five-speed transaxle, inboard rear brakes, de Dion rear
suspension, and a platform chassis – no modified Fiat
components for Pegaso: almost every part was made on the
premises regardless of cost. These were wonderful cars that
carried the symbol of Pegasus, the flying horse, unlike the
prancing horse of Ferrari with its feet still on the ground!

Most of Pegaso's cars had a 2.8-litre engine, although the
first four examples of the 99 made between 1951 and 1958
had 2.5-litre engines and the last three or four had less
complicated pushrod engines of up to 4.7 litres capacity.
Maserati increased the capacity of its road cars to 2 litres in
1951; Zagato and Frua bodies were built on the chassis
besides Pinin Farina's. In the meantime Ferrari, who like
Pegaso was producing only about one touring car per
month, increased the capacity of the Inter to 2.6 litres for
the 212 model with an alternative chassis in short wheelbase
form, called the Export. These cars used a V12 engine based
on a design by Gioacchino Colombo, who left in 1952 to
work for Maserati. Subsequently the capacity of these
touring Ferraris was increased to 3 litres for the Type 250,
which used another V12 engine designed by Colombo's
successor, Aurelio Lampredi, as its basis.

The first sports cars with this engine had been the Type
340 competition models of 1950, which were followed by
the Type 342 4.1-litre America grand tourer upon which all
the big touring Ferraris that followed were based! These
new large Ferraris had a stronger back axle and at the
same time received far higher ratios, with the result that the
top speed of some of the lightest models was in the
260 km/h (160 mph) class. Later, in 1953, the Lampredi
engine was linered down to 3 litres for the Type 250
Export, which shared the same chassis as the 375 America
with the 4.5-litre engine.

During these years, only one British manufacturer, apart
from Bentley with its Continental, had been remotely in the
exotic class. This was Jensen, who produced the Interceptor
powered by a 4-litre Austin engine in 1949. It was a
coachbuilt coupé more capable of effortless 145 km/h
(90 mph) cruising than ultimate performance. Bristol's 404
made in 1954 was a far superior car. Because of its short
wheelbase it was also one of the smallest built by the firm
from Filton. When fitted with the most powerful version of
Bristol's 2-litre engine it was capable of nearly 190 km/h
(120 mph) with good, if somewhat sensitive, handling. Like
the Bristol saloons, it was extremely well made and very
comfortable: a true Grand Tourer.

The magnificent Mercedes 300SL Gullwing coupé that
startled the world in 1952 and eventually went into
production in 1954 was in a class of its own. This fuel-
injected 3-litre lightweight, coil sprung coupé could reach
160 km/h (100 mph) from rest in only 16 seconds and
exceed 215 km/h (135 mph) on its best axle ratio. The only
problem with such a performance was that the braking was
scarcely adequate and the handling was as tricky as that of
the lower-powered Porsche, which shared similar swing
axles. In the hands of an expert it was fine, but driven by a
novice it could be decidedly dangerous because it was so
sensitive. Indeed, these cars were not to be treated lightly.

BMW was producing rivals for each car in the Mercedes
range at the time but, sadly, few of its 3.2-litre V8 Type 507

The Mercedes 300SL 'Gullwing', so called because of the ingenious way in which the doors opened, was at the time a very advanced car, with a spaceframe, fuel injection, all-independent suspension and beautifully streamlined body. Unfortunately the doors, well illustrated on this 1955 model, had to be abandoned because of the risk of jamming if the car overturned.

coupés were made because of financial problems. The 507s that did leave the Bavarian works were fantastic two-seaters with a top speed of around 210 km/h (130 mph).

With competitors such as these, Ferrari increased the capacity of its engines even more, to 4.9 litres, in company with its racing sports cars. This engine first appeared in a Type 410 Superamerica chassis in 1955, reputedly after Enzo Ferrari had said that he wanted an engine with each cylinder the size of a Chianti bottle!

As Ferrari was thinking big in its search for performance to leave its rivals standing, so were others, and Chrysler's excellent V8 had not escaped Ferrari's attention. The French had been able to list five exotic cars before the war, Bugatti, Delage, Delahaye, Hotchkiss and Lago-Talbot but, owing to the ravages of the Occupation and the subsequent French fiscal system, the survivors were hardly able to sell a handful of cars between them. Only Talbot produced any quantity of cars that might be deemed exotic after the war, and they were chiefly competition models rather than road-going machines.

The French exotics were practically extinct when industrialist Jean Daninos, who made family saloon car bodies as well as filing cabinets, revealed his dream of a French national car in 1954. True, it had a Chrysler engine, but a proper French engine could be used later, he declared patriotically. He based his magnificent new body on special coachwork he had built for a Bentley in 1951. Development continued through the Facel-bodied Ford Comète coupé to the definitive Facel Vega shape of 1954. This brave new luxury car had lovely lines, a tubular chassis with conventional suspension, and Chrysler push-button automatic transmission. A French-built manual gearbox was listed at great extra expense. The body, which was welded to the chassis for rigidity, was also notable for the extensive use of stainless steel for its brightwork, one of Facel's specialities. Performance was good, with a 200 km/h (125 mph) top speed, although the braking ability left a lot to be desired. The brakes were given power assistance in 1957 in an attempt to help them cope with the additional performance provided, as Chrysler's big engine became even larger and more powerful in the horsepower race on the other side of the Atlantic.

In Great Britain, Jensen hit the headlines by producing the first four-seater car to have glass-fibre coachwork. This was the 541 of 1953, which had many novel features, including a front end that hinged back in its entirety for access to the well-tried Austin engine, plus a swivelling radiator air intake shutter. The 541 had a new chassis to replace the old Austin-based cruciform, which improved the handling. This was welcome because the far lighter 541 was now capable of 180 km/h (112 mph), which was increased further by installing a higher-performance version of the engine later. Disc brakes were fitted all round with the 541 De Luxe of 1956.

By 1957, Enzo Ferrari was taking more interest in production cars, realizing that he could produce the 250 Europa on a regular basis and so help to support his racing activities. The overall dimensions of the Lampredi engine were too bulky for the 250 Europa, and so a revised version of the shorter and lighter Colombo unit was fitted from

---

The HK 500 of 1960 was probably the finest of the French Facel Vegas, because it had disc brakes and a very powerful American Chrysler hemi-head V8 engine which gave it a top speed of around 225 km/h (140 mph). The Facel Vega was also notable for the quality and beauty of its coachwork.

1954. The Lampredi-engined 410 Superamerica continued to be made with all manner of coachwork until 1959, eventually being offered with optional disc brakes as Ferrari lost his suspicion of this innovation. A lightweight version of the 410, named quite appropriately the Superfast, was marketed from 1956.

The 250 Europa became known simply as the 250 GT in 1957 and went into production with Pinin Farina or Scaglietti bodies. It was at this time that the Ferrari Berlinettas began to reach the height of their fame. Berlinetta means 'little sedan', or 'coupé', in Italian and over the years all Ferrari coupés had been dubbed Berlinettas. Now, however, with regular production of GT cars, the name Berlinetta began to have more significance: it was applied to the lightweight versions of the coupés rather than the heavier touring cars. Ironically, these raucous, and often spartan Berlinettas became even more popular after the appalling crash at Le Mans in 1955 in which 82 people were killed. It happened when an outright racing car, a Mercedes 300SLR, careered into the crowd following a collision with a much slower Austin-Healey 100S. There was a considerable reaction throughout the sport and races for Grand Touring cars of far more comparable performance were substituted; the lightweight Ferrari coupés proved ideal. Although these cars were intended mainly for competition they could still be driven on the road and, because of their mechanical similarity, cannot be divorced from the luxurious coupés.

Maserati, who with Mercedes and Jaguar had been Ferrari's chief track competitor, continued to produce its A6G/2000 in 1957 as the company developed the new 3500GT car. This had a new six-cylinder engine, designed purely for road work, with twin overhead camshafts that was similar in many respects to Jaguar's XK power unit, except that it had 12 sparking plugs. This was a popular feature on racing engines, but some people commented that perhaps it found favour with Maserati's proprietor, Count Adolfo Orsi, because he also made sparking plugs! The 3500GT had a four-speed gearbox and a tubular chassis with coil

spring suspension, although it retained a live rear axle. Touring took over from Allemano as the coachbuilder and fitted a lightweight body so that the 3500GT was capable of 210 km/h (130 mph). Unfortunately, its roadholding could be rather wild with its relatively unsophisticated chassis and suspension.

The 5-litre V8 Maserati coupé introduced two years later was far more formidable. It was essentially a 'beefed-up' 3500GT fitted with an engine that produced up to 400 bhp, or nearly twice the power of the 3.5-litre. The idea was to find a home for surplus racing engines and, in a straight line, the result was more than a match for Ferrari's biggest cars. A variety of coachbuilders supplied bodies, principally Allemano, and the customers included the Aga Khan and the Shah of Persia, as Iran was called then. When testing this amazing status symbol on roads near the factory in Modena, northern Italy, a top speed of more than 275 km/h (170 mph) was achieved!

Ferrari continued to manufacture the old 410 SA (Superamerica) or Superfast, but the 250 GT made at the same time sold well in far larger numbers. The short wheelbase Berlinettas became better and better, culminating in the Scaglietti-bodied versions of 1959–61. The larger and slower 250 GTs were then developed the other way with a two-plus-two seating configuration, following a Pininfarina prototype in 1960. This was called the 250 GTE and was followed by the most elegant Berlinetta of them all, the Lusso, in 1962.

This magnificent car was given a good run for its money by the Aston Martin DB4 which had been introduced in 1958 and was soon available in short wheelbase Berlinetta style as the DB4GT with an even more potent engine. These Aston Martins were extremely well made with a standard of finish and interior far better than those of their competitors.

By 1960, the Type 410 Ferraris with their Lampredi engines were starting to feel decidedly clumsy, so the top model became what was in effect a 250 GT chassis with a 4-litre engine derived from the Colombo unit. This was called the Type 400 Superamerica and could reach 300 km/h (186 mph) in its most potent and lightest form! At the same time, the maestro had an even more spectacular Ferrari built for himself. It was a short wheelbase version of the old 410 SA with a Pininfarina body, called the Superfast II, that was to set the style for the next batch of 400 Superamericas.

Facel Vega at last fitted disc brakes as standard in 1960 when the top speed of the HK500 was nudging 225 km/h (140 mph), thanks to an abundance of American horsepower. The reason that the company had been reluctant to do this earlier was because a large proportion of the car, and a disastrous and floppy four-door version called the Excellence, was already foreign and Daninos was still chasing his dream of an outstanding all-French exotic car. To a degree, he had achieved his ambition in 1959 when he had produced the Facellia, a scaled-down HK500 with a four-cylinder twin-cam hemi-head engine made at his works in Pont-à-Mousson. But sadly, it took until 1962 to rid the engine of teething troubles, by which time the money was running out. Various other engines were tried in place of this 1.5-litre unit, but none succeeded and the firm closed down in 1964.

That was the year when a British version of what the Facel Vega HK500 should have been finally went into production. This was the Gordon-Keeble which used a Chevrolet Corvette engine and transmission in a competent chassis with a stylish four-seater glass-fibre body by Bertone. It was only about three-quarters of the weight of a Facel and went just as fast, but at first the little Hampshire company could not cope with the demand and consequently orders then fell off. The Gordon-Keeble prototype had been

ABOVE *The Gordon Keeble, built in England between 1964 and 1967, was an ill-fated attempt at making a first-class GT car with a glass-fibre body. The performance with its Chevrolet V8 engine was exceptional because of its light weight, but problems in meeting the demand for the car led to the early demise of its makers.*

ABOVE RIGHT *The Maserati Mistral of 1964 was a very attractive GT car notable for its aggressive yet flowing lines. The frontal aspect of this design by Frua appeared in modified form on Alfa Romeos and ACs two years later, at the same time as the huge rear window inspired the distinctive styling of the new Jensen Interceptor.*

RIGHT *The 1974 Interceptor Mark III convertible was one of the most successful of Jensen's postwar designs, combining the searing performance of the standard fixed-head coupé with the delights of open-air motoring at its most luxurious. Sadly, however, the energy crisis led to the British firm's liquidation in 1976.*

around since 1960 and was an obvious threat to the similarly conceived Jensen, so the latter company revised the 541 in 1962 with a Chrysler engine and transmission like that of a Facel Vega or Bristol. The result was the Jensen CV8, which was as ugly as the Gordon-Keeble was good looking but, with its sumptuously furnished glass-fibre body, it was capable of more than 210 km/h (130 mph).

With this sort of competition, Maserati started updating the 3500GT. The first indication of this was the Sebring in 1962 which had a boxy bodywork by Vignale; and the second sign, which led to the demise of the 3500GT, was the handsome Mistral, which was one of Frua's most successful designs. The Sebring and Mistral (to adopt the spelling in the Maserati catalogue, although the badges often read Mistrale!) then received more power by courtesy of a 3.7-litre fuel-injected engine which also became available in 4-litre form for even greater, 225 km/h (140 mph) style, performance.

The two Maseratis sold well even as Ferrari brought in new cars to combat the menace of Lamborghini. The first of these was the 330 GT of 1964, which used a 4-litre version of the Colombo-based engine and gave good accommodation for four people with a maximum speed of more than 240 km/h (150 mph). It set new standards of smoothness and flexibility for a Ferrari, but still lacked refinement in the body compared with an Aston Martin. The British firm, meanwhile, had raised the engine capacity to 4-litres with the DB5, which was to gain fame as James Bond's car in the film *Goldfinger*.

Jensen set equally high standards with the bodywork of its new Interceptor introduced in 1966. It was mechanically similar to a CV8 but used a steel body styled by Vignale. One of the most distinctive features of the coachwork was the 'goldfish bowl' rear window, decidedly reminiscent of Frua's Maserati Mistral. A four-wheel-drive version of the Interceptor called the FF was introduced at the same time and was completely original in concept. It used automatic transmission as standard with Ferguson Formula four-wheel

drive and Dunlop Maxaret anti-locking brakes. The result was an incredibly sure-footed 210 km/h (130 mph) GT car of great luxury that remains an all-time classic.

It was hardly surprising that strong Mistral influences could also be seen in the Frua-designed bodywork of AC's new GT car, the 428, in 1968: essentially a luxurious version of this British company's established Cobra sports racing car described in the next chapter. Sufficient power was supplied by a lazy 7-litre Ford V8 to take this bulky beauty up to 225 km/h (140 mph).

Yet another exotic car of the late 1960s that shared a similar shape (and, it is thought, some of the panels) with the Mistral and AC 428 was the Monteverdi 375 built by a BMW garage in Switzerland. This four-seater GT powered by a Chrysler hemi-head V8 was built on a shoestring by enthusiast Peter Monteverdi with a tubular chassis that gave it exceptional straight-line stability all the way up to its 240 km/h (150 mph) maximum speed. The chief problem with these cars was that owners frequently had to do the development themselves. On one model the battery could only be changed after removing the engine!

The Italian refrigerator manufacturers Iso also produced exotic cars, on a slightly larger scale than Monteverdi. The most outstanding of these was the Iso Grifo. This spectacular, long, low GT car styled by Bertone was capable of around 240 km/h (150 mph) or more depending on the state of tune of its 5.3-litre Chevrolet V8 engine.

The cars of the inventive Argentinian enthusiast Alejandro de Tomaso used to be built in Italy in a similar way to the Iso and Monteverdi until his fantastic Ford V8-powered Mangusta surprised everybody in 1967. This extraordinary mid-engined machine had a body designed by Ghia with gullwing doors for access to the engine compartment. The result, with its 'wings' raised, looked like some evil bird of prey. It gripped the imagination of Ford of America, who helped put it into much larger scale production. However, it lacked development and proved to have roadholding that was, to put it mildly, 'exciting'. This

RIGHT *The Ferrari 275 GTB, illustrated here in 1967 two-cam, six-carburettor form, was one of the last of the great front-engined GT cars produced by the famous Italian firm. This roadgoing coupé was also eminently suitable for competition with its 280 bhp engine and rear-mounted five-speed gearbox.*
BELOW *The awe-inspiring de Tomaso Mangusta of 1967 had enormous potential performance and an ultra-short wheelbase. It won the support of the American Ford company but it proved to be an impractical product because of very difficult handling problems.*

de Tomaso was much improved when it was redesigned by former Ferrari, Maserati and Lamborghini engineer Gianpaolo Dallara. Other small-scale productions from Italy included the Bizzarrini GT Strada 5300, which bore a close resemblance to the Iso Grifo and could manage a top speed of 278 km/h (174 mph).

These cars were all classics in their way with spectacular lines and masses of power from their American V8 engines,

but none had the finesse of Ferrari's 275 GTB Berlinetta, which was also available in open, or Spider, 275 GTS form. This car, which was introduced in 1965, had a 3.3-litre V12 engine in the front and a five-speed transaxle at the back, with independent suspension all round. Later versions were further improved by fitting a torque tube between the engine and transaxle, and really took off when their single overhead camshaft engines received twin cams on each bank. They were splendid cars with exceptional responsiveness in all departments. Meanwhile, the 250 GT was uprated to become the 330 GT with a 4-litre engine.

In 1965 Aston Martin brought out the DB6, with larger rear seats and improved aerodynamics which decreased lift at the maximum speed of around 240 km/h (150 mph). Aston Martin also widened the platform chassis in 1967 in anticipation of a new four overhead camshaft V8 engine, and fitted new bodywork along the lines established by rivals such as Ferrari, Maserati and AC. This new model, the DBS, was produced rather hurriedly to boost flagging sales in Great Britain, which had been hit by a credit squeeze. As a result the chassis platform was on the heavy side because it lacked the many months of development that would have been needed to reduce weight without impairing strength. The new V8 engine had to have extensive development to make it reliable, so the existing six-cylinder engine was used initially in the DBS. As a result, this heavy car felt underpowered compared to previous Aston Martins.

In the larger exotic class Ferrari's biggest car, a new Superfast called the 500, had been introduced a year earlier, in 1964. It had a new 4.9-litre V12 and considerably smoother lines than those of earlier models and, as a result, it was no sluggard, being capable of 278 km/h (174 mph).

By this time, Lamborghini was well into its stride with the 350GT and 400GT and dominated the 1966 season by producing the amazing mid-engined Miura with a 4-litre V12 engine mounted transversely and driving through a gearbox that even had synchromesh on reverse, as Feruccio Lamborghini was of the opinion that it should be possible to change into any gear while moving! The front-engined saloon car, the Espada, was followed by an interim 260 km/h (160 mph) GT car called the Islero before the two-plus-two seater Jarama was introduced in 1970. This was a magnificent modern-styled machine which, with the well-tried V12 engine and excellent suspension, put everything else except Ferrari and Aston Martin in the shade. When the Aston Martin DBS eventually received its 5.3-litre all-alloy V8 engine in 1969 it was transformed into a really high-performance exotic car capable of the magic 260 km/h (160 mph). Without a doubt, for finish and comfort, Aston Martin coachwork still left the Italians behind. The DBS V8 was marred only by a sometimes temperamental fuel-injection system. In an attempt to keep pace with its great rival, Aston Martin, Jensen had updated the Interceptor and FF into Mark II form with detail refinements, mainly to the interior.

Maserati had continued to produce beautiful and reliable GT cars, now powered by the company's own V8 engine; they suffered from having an old-fashioned solid rear axle.

Maseratis of this period were the Ghibli, designed by Ghia, and introduced in 1966, which was one of the most beautiful GT cars ever made and no mean performer with a 4.7-litre engine; the Mexico, which was phased out for the Quattroporte; and the four-seater Indy, designed by Vignale to offer more accommodation than the Ghibli. One of the main advantages of these cars was that they needed relatively little specialized maintenance and were much more reliable than the products of some of the smaller manufacturers.

All these cars had classic virtues, but none really combined them to the same degree as Ferrari's 4.4-litre 365 series introduced in 1967. These cars bore a closer resemblance to the 500 Superfast than Ferrari's 330 GT. At first they were luxurious two-plus-two seaters with power steering, air conditioning, a single overhead cam V12 and independent suspension all round. Then the greatest of them all, the 365 GTB four-cam Daytona, a two-seater coupé in the best Berlinetta traditions, appeared in 1968. This 278 km/h (174 mph) car, which later became available

RIGHT *The Ghibli was undoubtedly the most beautiful front-engined Maserati GT car ever made, with superb smooth lines and luxurious coachwork. The Ghibli, with its V8 engine, had an excellent performance and got a reputation for extreme durability and relatively low running costs because of its simple 'live' rear axle.*
BELOW *The Lamborghini Espada, produced from 1967, is among the world's fastest four-seater cars, with a long, low, body and powerful four overhead camshaft V12 front-mounted engine. The Espada is so well engineered that it has been called the Rolls-Royce of GT cars.*

in open form, was the last great front-engined GT that Ferrari built before going over to mid-engined machinery like the Dino 206 GT of 1969. Then, with Fiat's help, the Dino 246 GT was developed with a steel body for larger-scale production in 1970. It had a 2.4-litre V6 engine mounted amidships in one of the most pleasing bodies seen for years. As to be expected with the weight distributed so evenly the handling was superb. Lamborghini produced what was potentially an even more exciting model, the 2.5-litre V8-engined Urraco, which was capable of 240 km/h (150 mph), to combat this new Ferrari. Sadly, however, this small Lamborghini lacked development, although it was improved later by fitting a 3-litre engine. Lamborghini's resources had been directed towards perfecting a spectacular replacement for the Miura in 1972: this was the Countach. It was an eye-catching mid-engined car, with 'butterfly-wing' doors, which could hit 300 km/h (186 mph) with its 4-litre V12 engine and because of its improved aerodynamics and roadholding was far easier to drive than

the Miura. Monteverdi tried to match Lamborghini with the squat mid-engined Hai, powered by a 7-litre Chrysler V8, but it was not remotely in the same class.

Fiat had been struggling to sell a top-of-the-range saloon since 1969. This was the 130, Fiat's first car to be designed without cost in mind. Everything was new from the floorpan upwards: it had independent suspension all round and disc brakes all round to give excellent handling and roadholding. A Ferrari-style single overhead cam V6 engine was used, initially in the tax-dodging 2.8-litre size. This did not produce enough torque for the automatic transmission, so the capacity was increased in 1971 to 3.2 litres, even at the expense of putting the car into a new tax class. The new engine produced more than enough power to haul this opulent saloon up to 190 km/h (120 mph), but it still did not sell well because of its fussy, rather old-fashioned styling. The BMWs, Mercedes and Jaguars looked more attractive and performed as well, if not better. But Fiat would not give in and commissioned Pininfarina to produce

a really beautiful body for the 130. The result was one of the most striking cars ever produced by Fiat, the 130 coupé of 1971. It made the big Fiat look like a Ferrari, or at least a Lancia. In this form, the Fiat 130 coupé must rate among the more exclusive classics, as only small numbers were made at quite a high price. They were real gems and the forerunners of a new generation of GTs from Ferrari.

Throughout the years, Porsche's products had verged on the exotic until the company made its cars even more exclusive. In 1971 Porsche increased the capacity of the flat six-cylinder single overhead camshaft air-cooled engine used in the 911 from 2.2 to 2.4 litres. The 911 represented a triumph of perfectionism over difficult design. When the Porsche family laid out their sports car in 1947, they put the engine behind the rear axle line to allow the maximum amount of room for passengers within the short wheelbase. That was where it stayed right through the 356s and into the 911s introduced in 1964. The weight of the engine caused the car's tail to swing round very quickly on cornering and led to 'interesting' handling, which could be exploited by an expert driver but could cause serious problems for somebody less experienced. However, by

The Dino 246 GT coupé was a particularly good-looking Ferrari, with its delightfully slim and rounded bodywork. It also performed like a firecracker with a screaming 2.4-litre V6 engine and handled beautifully because the engine was mounted in the centre.

continuous development, including using exotic light alloys to reduce the weight of the engine and its transaxle, these tendencies were suppressed to such an extent that the Porsche 911 had become a much easier car to drive in 1968. It was still powered by a very small engine, however, and lacked the ultimate relaxed performance of a true exotic car. Then the engine's size was gradually increased until, with the advent of the best model, the 1971 2.4-litre 911S, the 911 was really in the supercar class. Its price had always been high, and this had been rising dramatically as well. These 225 km/h (140 mph) Porsches were manufactured with great care and, because of their race-bred engineering, were far more reliable than any of the other exotic cars. As the 911's performance increased so were the sales of the smaller manufacturers reduced. These smaller firms were badly hit by the oil crisis of 1973, after which few other than established makers like Ferrari could contemplate producing exotic cars in any quantity.

Porsche carried on decimating the sales of its rivals by bringing out a much faster variant of the 911, the 2.7-litre Carrera RS, in 1972. This car, complete with duck's tail spoiler at the back and frontal air dam for better handling, could reach 250 km/h (155 mph). Even its roadholding was by now tenacious, thanks to the great strides made in tyre technology. It was the first sign of a change in policy for the German giant. For years Porsche had produced extraordinary racing cars, culminating in the 917, which dominated sports car racing from 1970. The development needed to keep this 370 km/h (230 mph) car at the top, including turbocharging, was very expensive and the 917 bore little resemblance to anything that could be driven on the road. Therefore Porsche decided to cut costs and concentrate on competition with road-based cars, such as the 911. Because the Carrera RS was so similar to a standard 911, it could be ordered with the full complement of luxurious fittings, making it a formidable exotic car. Sales soared predictably.

Alfa Romeo had a half-hearted attempt to follow suit with the front-engined Montreal coupé of 1973, which used a 2.5-litre engine based on the one installed in a racing car. It was fast but lacked the finesse of a Porsche.

In 1969 Citroën had bought a major share in Maserati and the first fruits of this were seen in the production of the mid-engined Bora of 1971. This magnificent beast, built

ABOVE *The Panther J72, of which a 1979 model is illustrated, was based unashamedly on the prewar Jaguar SS100 sports car. With its high performance (as a result of using modern Jaguar running gear) and superb lines, it sold well to those in search of a nostalgic trip into the past.*
LEFT *The 1973 Porsche Carrera RS 2.7-litre was, without a doubt, one of the best of the early 911 series. It was built mostly in ultra-lightweight form for competition and as such could achieve 250 km/h (155 mph) with stupendous acceleration. Later, American bumper regulations and a change of policy within the company led to heavier 911s that lacked the same taut appeal.*

along the lines of a Miura, was powered by a 4.7-litre V8 and used Citroën hydraulics. It could reach 260 km/h (160 mph) easily and is still one of the greatest exotic cars.

One of the principal reasons for Citroën's interest in Maserati was that a high-output engine was needed for the French company's new exotic car, the SM. This sleek four-seater had very advanced technology, coupled with outstanding handling, as was to be expected of Citroën, and was powered by a Maserati 2.6-litre V6 engine. This gave it a top speed of 220 km/h (137 mph) with good economy, thanks to Citroën's splendid streamlining. This engine was first fitted to a Bora in 1972 to make the Maserati Merak and was later used in 2.9-litre form when the Italian firm was left with a stockpile as the partnership floundered. Despite dramatic attempts to reduce the weight of the Merak it has always stayed in the shadow of the Bora.

As manufacturers such as Maserati and Ferrari adopted a mid-engined layout and used more and more advanced technology, they left a gap for exotic replicas of the past. The best of these, the Panther J72 of 1972, built by fashion designer Bob Jankel at Byfleet, Surrey, and given a Jaguar XK engine, was a sports car in the prewar SS Jaguar idiom. As production of this nostalgic machine increased, Jaguar V12 engines were fitted to give a formidable straight-line

performance, even if the handling could be distinctly 'antique'. A gigantic saloon inspired by the Bugatti Royale was also built from 1975.

There was no looking back for Ferrari, however, as the firm continued to produce its large front-engined GT cars and built a striking new mid-engined model, the Berlinetta Boxer, in 1971. This two-seater, with Pininfarina bodywork, was called a Boxer because of its horizontally opposed flat 12-cylinder engine of 4.4 litres capacity. Each bank of pistons 'boxed' the other. With the best part of 400 bhp, this 365 BB was capable of more than 290 km/h (180 mph), putting it in the Countach class.

Porsche continued to develop the 911 and eventually changed the type number to 930, which represented the company's top model in 1975. This was what amounted to a production version of the Carrera RSR racer with a very luxurious interior and a turbocharged version of the Porsche 3-litre flat-six engine. The years of development on the 917 had not been wasted as this was the most controllable turbocharged car, and it put Porsche on a pinnacle among exotic car makers. The 260 km/h (160 mph) 930 continued into the 1980s with better brakes and a 3.3-litre engine as a new front-engined 4.5-litre V8 water-cooled Porsche GT car was developed. This was the 928 of 1977, which was to have replaced the long-lived 911s. However, the 911s remained so popular that the 928, which offered a similar standard of performance and comfort, was sold alongside the 930 and more mundane 911s.

Ferrari increased the capacity of its Berlinetta Boxer to 5 litres to counter the Porsche 930's great flexibility, at the same time continuing with the smaller V6- and V8-engined Dinos, which looked very much like scaled-down Berlinetta Boxers. These were the wedge-shaped 308 GT4 of 1974 designed by Bertone with a 3-litre V8 engine and the far more attractive Pininfarina 308 GTB built from 1975 with a similar engine. This king of exotic car makers continued to develop the front-engined cars with V12 power, and even with automatic transmission for the 400 GT of 1977. These larger Ferraris showed strong Fiat 130 influences.

Maserati planned the Khamsin to replace the Ghibli in 1974 but its launch was delayed, first by the oil crisis and then with the splitting up of the partnership with Citroën in 1975. Alejandro de Tomaso then managed to borrow

The Porsche Turbo (930) of 1979 shown here is the ultimate development of the 911-based road cars. Its 260 km/h (160 mph) plus performance and superb engineering makes it more practical than most exotic cars to run. The Turbo is also a particularly comfortable Porsche, with a high level of interior fittings.

enough money from the Italian government to take over Maserati and continue producing his own cars now that the Ford company was moving away from its partnership with him. He found, however, that the old-established Italian firm, with Count Orsi back at the helm, was effectively taking over design aspects of the existing de Tomasos. Meanwhile the Khamsin was introduced bearing all the signs of the Citroën era in that it inherited the SM's hydraulic system. The all-independent suspension was pure Maserati, as opposed to hydraulic Citroën, but use had been made of this form of power assistance to provide a light clutch pedal. Surprisingly, this was to be the only supercar to have this feature. The rivals – most of whom even extended power assistance to their radio aerials – somehow ignored this obvious feature, being content to supply cars with clutches made extremely heavy because of the strong units needed to absorb the great power of their engines. With a 5-litre version of the Maserati V8 engine, the Khamsin was far more of a two-seater coupé than a two-plus-two. It was good for 260 km/h (160 mph), with excellent handling endowed by its very rigid tubular chassis combined with a steel floorpan and soft suspension.

The first signs of the de Tomaso collaboration were seen in the Maserati Kyalami two-plus-two introduced soon after. The history of this exotic coupé was fascinating, dating back to the time of Ford's involvement with de Tomaso. The first intention had been to produce a car for

Ford of America that could compete with the existing Mercedes 450SLC coupé. By the time de Tomaso had designed the car, Ford was opting out of its involvement with the Argentinian's firm, retaining only its interest in the associated Ghia coachworks. De Tomaso then simply called the new Ford, which had been based in part on the existing de Tomaso Deauville (in turn influenced by the Jaguar XJ6), the de Tomaso Longchamps. This car, which looked remarkably like a Mercedes 450SLC, retained the Ford V8 engine (shared with the de Tomaso Pantera) for which it had been designed. When de Tomaso merged with Maserati, the Maserati 4.2-litre V8 was substituted and, with minor restyling, the result was the Maserati Kyalami. It was more exclusive than the Mercedes 450SLC and more pleasing to drive, and held the road better than the other mass-produced rival, the BMW CSi. It was not quite so refined, however, as the Jaguar XJ coupé (or XJC) based on the Jaguar XJ6 and XJ12, to which it traces its inspiration.

Jaguar entered this field wholeheartedly in 1975 with a striking new two-plus-two coupé, the XJ-S, using many of the components of the XJ12 saloon and coupé. The XJ-S was a superb car, enjoying relatively high sales and appearing to be well set for production deep into the 1980s. Aston Martin survived financial crisis after financial crisis to uprate the performance of the V8 with a Vantage unit, which kept it on a par with the Porsches and Ferraris. The company also bravely produced a spectacular new wedge-shaped saloon, the Lagonda, with four full seats and styling that was among the most striking ever seen. At first, in 1976, this space-age creation used highly sophisticated electronic controls, but problems with production held it back three years. And then it had ordinary switches; but it was still one of the best-looking machines on the road.

Bristol placed itself firmly in the exotic car price bracket with the 412 convertible, an updated 411, and the new 603 saloon which became available in economy or high-performance, 250 km/h (150 mph), trim. The chief rival for this, apart from the Lagonda and Jaguar XJ12, was a Series Two version of the Maserati Quattroporte, which was rather like an amalgam of all known Maserati and de Tomaso parts in a four-door shell. Lamborghini floundered in financial crisis, too, producing a new 3-litre open car, the Silouette, alongside the existing Urraco. The Silouette was a dramatically restyled Urraco, with chassis redesigned to use Pirelli's sensational new P7 tyres, which endowed it with magnificent roadholding. The Countach's chassis was redeveloped at the same time in Countach S form.

Finally, and most expensive of all, Rolls-Royce introduced the Camargue in 1975. This was a special version of the Corniche using a body designed by Pininfarina and built by Mulliner, Park Ward with absolutely no regard to cost. In fact its price, which was nearly £40,000 on introduction, was so high that it became an instant status symbol: a true exotic.

COMPETITION CARS

ABOVE *A tiny Scotsman called Archie Scott-Brown, who had a deformed hand and foot, overcame these handicaps to work wonders at the wheel of a fearsome Lister-Jaguar like the one shown here. He became a highly respected and successful driver in the late 1950s. These cars still dominate historic sports car racing today.*
RIGHT *The Aston Martins of the late 1950s and early 1960s were rightly called the Englishman's Ferrari, particularly the most exciting of them all, the ultra-lightweight DB4GT with coachwork by Zagato. This is one of the rare 1962 examples which were raced by such drivers as world champion-to-be Jim Clark.*

Throughout the postwar period, classic cars have been influenced by competition models, particularly in the early years when it was possible to drive a racing car on the road providing it was equipped with wings and lighting of some form. And some of these road-going competition cars have been classics, of course. Probably the greatest of them all was the 1954 Jaguar D type, which led directly to the production Jaguar E type sports car that caused such a sensation in 1961. The Allard J2X competition model built in the early 1950s gave rise, indirectly, to one of the world's most exciting sports cars, the AC Cobra, in 1962.

The thundering Allards from London had their Cadillac or Chrysler V8 engines installed in America to avoid import restrictions and became the first such Anglo-American hybrids in competition. Because of their light weight – they had narrow bodies with cycle-type wings on a tubular chassis – and masses of horsepower, their acceleration was tremendous. It did not matter very much that the cars were not particularly aerodynamic and their top speed was relatively low in relation to their power-to-weight ratio. They reached maximum speed much more quickly than most cars and as a result spent more time going fast on short circuits of the type that were becoming popular all over the world, particularly in America where their chief market lay.

The Talbot-Lago that raced with success in the same era was based on a prewar design. It used a 4.5-litre six-cylinder engine with two camshafts that gave it sufficient power to beat some Grand Prix cars over longer distances when its cycle-type wings and minimal lighting equipment were stripped off.

The Healey Silverstone produced from 1949 was based on the earlier Healey saloons and relied on Riley for more than

inspiration: it used the 2.5-litre engine, gearbox and rear axle from the British sports saloon. This cycle-winged sports car produced more than 100 bhp and proved ideal for long-distance rallying and circuit racing. It remains one of the firm's most desirable products. Frazer-Nash, of Isleworth, West London, produced a car on similar lines that was even more versatile. It started life as the High-Speed model in 1948 and was developed into the Le Mans Replica after finishing third in that great French race in 1949. This car, built to special order, was a dual-purpose Formula 2 and sports car that could also be used, little altered and with great success, in rallying. Later examples of this marque used all-enveloping bodies as cycle-type wings were outlawed from international competition in 1952. They gained in top speed but lost out on charm.

The Ferraris of the early postwar years were closely related to the production models, of course, with most competition Ferraris using either Berlinetta or Spider (open) bodywork. This depended on whether the event entered was a long-distance one, where the streamlining of the coupé's top might have been an advantage in that it would have given a higher top speed and reduced driver fatigue, or on tight, tough, circuits where the lighter weight and better visibility of the Spider would have been best.

The early postwar Aston Martins were built using the same principles; the DB2, built from 1950, achieved great success in long-distance racing and international rallying in practically standard form. Open versions with a special chassis, designed along the lines of the Jowett Jupiter by Eberan von Eberhorst, were raced with similar, but more highly tuned engines. The lessons learned from tuning these power units were seen in Vantage, or high-performance, versions of the standard cars. These racing Aston Martins were the DB3 and DB3S, which sometimes had a coupé top for races such as Le Mans, and was one of the best-looking

WMC 181

FAR LEFT *An era ended when Dan Gurney drove the last of the brutal front-engined sports cars, a 4.7-litre AC Cobra, into eighth place in the last of the world's great road races, the Targa Florio, in 1964. The famous race in Sicily was won by a Porsche 904, an early representative of the GT cars that took over from the traditional sports cars.*
LEFT *The Frazer-Nash Le Mans Replica was one of the last sports racing cars produced with cycle-type wings, before this style of bodywork was banned from international competition in 1952 as being too much like an outright racing car. However, the Bristol-engined Frazer-Nash was equally successful on the road.*

Astons ever made. Later versions of the DB3S were used to develop suspension systems and other aspects of design for the DB4; the DBR2 was used to develop the DB4's engine.

Jaguar also followed this line of development with the C type, which won at Le Mans in 1951 and 1953. The C type proved invaluable for development on the XK sports cars, and the results could even be seen in the Jaguar saloon cars, particularly in their engines. It also helped pioneer the use of disc brakes, which were of benefit to all cars for years to come. Meanwhile, the smaller classes of sports car racing featured cars such as the Cooper-MGs and Cooper-Bristols, which used a tubular chassis and transverse leaf spring independent suspension. With a simple lightweight body, they were to set trends that were reflected in sports cars for a decade and led to the AC Ace of 1954 and eventually to the Cobra.

The Jaguar D type was a very different car, having been devised by aircraft designer Malcolm Sayer. It was not surprising that it was like an aircraft, with a monocoque, or centre section, that resembled a fuselage. Because of its superior aerodynamics it was far faster than the C type and the lessons learned from this immortal design, which won at Le Mans three years running from 1955 to 1957, were to influence more than just Jaguar. The D type saw its final development in the lightweight E type sports car that raced in the early 1960s, managing fourth place at Le Mans in 1962.

This car was driven by the millionaire Briggs Cunningham, whose machines had been the best of the American racers of the early 1950s. His Cunninghams were hardly scientific, although they did try water-cooled drum

LEFT *The Jaguar D type designed in 1954, with aerodynamic coachwork by Malcolm Sayer who had worked on Bristol aircraft, became one of Britain's greatest sports racing cars, winning at Le Mans three times in a row. This example is one of a number raced by Duncan Hamilton, a former test pilot who was known for his heroic feats at the wheel of the D type.*

BELOW *A revolution started in sports car racing in 1955 when Colin Chapman introduced the ultra-lightweight Bristol-powered Lotus Mark 10 which, despite its diminutive size, ran rings around the big front-engined sports cars that had dominated this form of racing since the turn of the century.*

The 1955 Mercedes 300SLR was a sports racer
based on the W196 Grand Prix car. Its straight eight,
fuel-injected 3-litre engine developed almost 300 bhp. This
example in the Mercedes-Benz museum proudly bears the number 722:
the time at which it left Brescia on the morning of 1 May
1955 with Stirling Moss at the wheel to win the Mille
Miglia road race around Italy.

brakes, but they certainly helped hasten development of the great American V8s.

The Mercedes-Benz 300SLR built in 1952 was exactly the opposite. It was the forerunner of the fabulous 300SL Gullwing and used the straight eight-cylinder engine from the successful Mercedes-Benz Grand Prix cars of the 1950s. Like the Jaguar D type, the Mercedes, which won Le Mans in 1952, spawned a brand-new line of cars that anybody could buy, providing they had the money. And the 4.9-litre Ferrari that won the 24-hour event in 1954 led to the big Ferrari GT cars of the years to come.

In the smaller classes, the Porsche sports cars were being developed with the four-cam engine that was to find its way into road-going coupés in the Carrera models from 1955. It was in this period that lightweight versions of the four-cylinder Austin-Healey were being built, called the 100S, which remain one of the most outstanding products of the Warwick firm.

The Lotus Mark 6 that first appeared in 1952 was eventually put into production in modified form as the Lotus Seven in 1958. It proved to be such a success that the design is still being made today by Lotus dealers, Caterham Cars; it provides fantastic fun for a generation of enthusiasts hardly out of their cots at the time it was conceived. The suspension systems of later streamlined Lotus sports racing cars found their way on to such road cars as the beautiful Elite of 1957.

As development of the Elite was under way, Colin Chapman's little firm was already establishing its name in international competition with the Lotus Mark 8s, 9s, 10s and Elevens made in varying forms from 1956 to 1958. These ultra-lightweight and beautifully streamlined racers were built on the principle of making a car as light as possible and then strengthening it where it breaks rather than building a heavyweight and paring off weight bit by bit: a practice that has been adopted by competition car makers ever since.

Another superbly designed racing car was the Ferrari 250 Testa Rossa, winner at Le Mans in 1958. This influenced the design of the great GT cars to come from the Italian aristocrats and was called the Testa Rossa, or red head, because of the red crackle finish on its cam covers. Red is Italy's racing colour and the traditional hue of a Ferrari; it is also accepted as the colour of the very best engine, and the Testa Rossa was all of that.

One of the Ferrari's chief competitors in short-circuit racing was the lightweight Lister-Jaguar, with a tubular chassis built by a Cambridge agricultural engineering works and powered by a Jaguar D type engine. Occasionally these

ABOVE *The Ferrari Testa Rossa was developed from the old 2-litre Mondial in 1956 to fit in with the new capacity limits on big sports car racing. It was an immediate success and was powered by engines varying in size from 2 to 4 litres. Clearly shown in this photograph of the V12 unit are the two Marelli distributors (on left), the six Weber twin-choke carburettors and the famous red finish on the camshaft covers*
LEFT *The Mini-Cooper S was one of the most spectacular rally and track cars of the 1960s and early 1970s, using a variety of engines from 997 cc to 1275 cc. Shown here is the car with which Paddy Hopkirk won the 1964 Monte Carlo Rally.*

cars had a 'knobbly' body of the smallest dimensions and sometimes a bulbous aerodynamic body designed by Frank Costin, who was to go on to Marcos via Maserati. But, in whatever form, the Lister-Jaguars were to stay in action for years. Today they have reached new glories as the most successful cars in historic racing alongside the Ferrari Dino Grand Prix cars of the same era.

As these cars were fighting it out on the circuits, production sports cars were excelling in rallying. There were none more spectacular than the Big Healeys that battled with the Triumph TRs. Nobody who has ever seen one will forget the sound and the fury of a works-entered Austin-Healey 3000 storming up and down the rough roads of the Alps, through the duststorms of the Liège-Rome-Liège rally, or along forest tracks in off-road events. Almost all the development for the Austin-Healey line of sports cars was done on these machines, including increasing the engine capacity, which affected not only the sports cars but the saloons that shared their power unit.

The place of these great sports cars was finally usurped by the incredibly adaptable Minis, which were continually developed through Cooper and Cooper S form to dominate the smaller classes in saloon car racing and to win international rallies outright. The sight of fiercely duelling Minis screaming into corners side by side with their tyres smoking rekindled the enthusiasm of racing crowds everywhere. It also sold cars by the million as the Minis won the Monte Carlo and numerous other big rallies. However, what really captured the imagination of spectators was that the Minis were so small; it was almost like a David and Goliath contest with everybody on the side of the underdog. As it happened the 'underdog' was of far more advanced design and that is why it won. The countless lessons learned from these cars were to benefit the British Motor Corporation for many years.

One of the Mini's chief opponents was the Ford Cortina developed by Lotus, who was Cooper's great rival with Ferrari and BRM in Grand Prix racing at the time. These